Sylvanus Stall, Mary Wood-Allen

What a Young Girl Ought to Know

Sylvanus Stall, Mary Wood-Allen

What a Young Girl Ought to Know

ISBN/EAN: 9783337219499

Printed in Europe, USA, Canada, Australia, Japan

Cover: Foto ©Lupo / pixelio.de

More available books at **www.hansebooks.com**

Commendations from Eminent Men and Women

What a Young Girl Ought to Know

WHAT EMINENT PEOPLE IN AMERICA SAY.

FRANCES E. WILLARD.

Late President World's and National Woman's Christian Temperance Union.

"'What a Young Girl Ought to Know' is embodied in the little book of that name by Dr. Mary Wood-Allen, Superintendent of the Purity Work of the National W. C. T. U., and Rev. Sylvanus Stall, D.D. Among the many indications of the age that are full of encouragement to the reformer, none outranks the quickened interest of our people in teaching the young those sacred 'origins' which, above everything, they ought to know, and because of their ignorance of which thousands are marred in their moral being who might have been strong, pure, and happy. I do earnestly hope that this book, founded on a strictly scientific, but not forgetting a strong ethical basis, may be well known and widely read by the dear girls in their teens and the young women in their homes."

WHAT EMINENT PEOPLE IN AMERICA SAY.

AMELIA YEOMANS, M.D.
Vice-President Dominion W. C. T. U.

"'What a Young Girl Ought to Know' constitutes a contribution to preventive social purity literature for which the public may well be grateful.

"Fortified by purity born of knowledge, and inwrought with reverence for the Maker and His works, our daughters will, by such instruction, be prepared for a high and holy motherhood, and what is put in the mothers must reappear in the men and women of the future.

"I would advise mothers to obtain this book, studying it carefully themselves before placing it in the hands of their daughters."

MRS. KATHARINE LENTE STEVENSON.
Corresponding Secretary National W. C. T. U.

"There can hardly be too many additions to the line of literature which touches the vital problem of life in its relation to the young, provided that literature be of the right kind. The Vir Publishing Company has just issued 'What a Young Girl Ought to Know,' Mary Wood-Allen, M.D., and Sylvanus Stall, D.D., as its collaborators. The book, as might be expected from such authorship, is strong, direct, pure, as healthy as a breeze from the mountain top. It cannot fail to bring inspiration and a new ideal of life to the young girl who may read it. Its statement of facts is clear and delicate. It is a book which any mother may safely put into the hands of her daughter. We hail its advent as another harbinger of the day which is dawning when 'better manners, purer laws,' and a higher conception of life shall be the birthright of all."

MRS. ISABELLA MACDONALD ALDEN.
"Pansy," the Eminent Author.

"'What a Young Girl Ought to Know' is a book that mothers cannot afford to be without. It is just the book needed to teach what most people do not know how to teach, being scientific yet simple, and plain-spoken yet delicate. 'Blessed are the pure in heart,' said the Master, and blessed must they be who enforce this teaching.''

MRS. E. M. WHITTEMORE.

Founder of the Door of Hope, New York City.

"Most heartily should this little book, 'What a Young Girl Ought to Know,' be endorsed, not only for its purity of thought, but for the great tact and wisdom used in so delicately handling a matter of such sacred import, and may God indeed bless it far and wide. Especially may He bless it to young mothers in aiding them to more fully realize their solemn responsibility in the training of their children, and in like purity enable them thus to unfold all necessary knowledge pertaining to that which naturally appears so mysterious to the mind of a child. By so doing God will be honored, and the little ones spared later on from receiving erroneous and evil impressions from associates, which so repeatedly result in such disastrous experiences and sorrow."

MRS. ELIZABETH B. GRANNIS.

President National Christian League for the Promotion of Social Purity.

"I have been deeply interested in reading your book, 'What a Young Girl Ought to Know.' These facts ought to be judiciously brought to the intelligence of every child whenever it asks questions concerning its own origin. I have greatly enjoyed the simplicity of your statements and illustrations. I would that every parent might read this volume with their children, and manifest sufficient intimate acquaintance with them to answer every honest query of the child with a frankness similar to that which you have shown in writing these letters."

MRS. EMILY D. BOUTON.

Author of "Health and Beauty," "Social Etiquette," "House and Domestic Decorations," "Life's Gateways and How to Win Real Success," etc.

"I have just finished reading your book, 'What a Young Girl Ought to Know,' and no words are too strong to use in expressing my appreciation of its excellence. It simply *cannot* fail of its purpose—that of giving young girls an insight into their own nature and the laws of their being, and showing them how to preserve their physical and moral health and purity. You have written with such tenderness, such delicacy, and withal such an understanding of the young creatures who are facing the solemn mysteries of wifehood and motherhood, that your words must reach their hearts and influence their character for good. I can most heartily commend the book to every mother as one to place fearlessly in the hands of her daughters, to teach them of what is too often wrapped in a silence that seems to cover something vulgar and shameful, instead of that which should be regarded as pure and sacred."

HARRIET LINCOLN COOLIDGE.

Editor of "Trained Motherhood;" author of "In the Story Land," "Kindergarten Stories," "Talks to Mothers," "The Model Nursery."

"If every mother had read this beautiful book, entitled 'What a Young Girl Ought to Know,' there would not be so many heartaches in the world to-day. It is a book that mothers and daughters ought to own, and mothers who do not understand the *best* way to instruct their girls in the proper care of the body will find it clearly shown in this little volume. It contains a series of 'Twilight Talks,' in one of which Dr. Allen shows the purpose of her book by quoting these words of Geo. Macdonald: 'I want to help you to grow as beautiful as God meant you to be when he first thought of you,' and this book *does* help in the best and purest way."

MRS. FRANCES SHELDON BOLTON.
Editor of "Mothers' Journal."

"No intelligent, thoughtful mother of young children can afford to be without Dr. Mary Wood-Allen's last book, entitled, 'What a Young Girl Ought to Know.'"

JENNIE B. MERRILL, Ph.D.

Supervisor of Kindergartens, New York City.

"I have followed with growing interest Dr. Wood-Allen's writings and lectures on these subjects for years, and consider that in them are to be found the safest counsel for parents and teachers—for teachers have a duty in these lines of instruction as well as parents. Permit me to add that, in my opinion, the wisest parents will read and digest the book, and teach 'here a little and there a little,' while the child is not only young but *very young*. But if parents are not equal to this pleasant duty, the book can be read directly to the child at ten or twelve years of age, or it would not be amiss, at that age, to give the book to the child."

IRA D. SANKEY.

The world-famed Gospel Singer.

"Every mother in the land that has a daughter should secure for her a copy of 'What a Young Girl Ought to Know.' It will save the world untold sorrow."

WM. H. KINNICUTT.

Physical Director Y. M. C. A., Cleveland, Ohio.

"While eminently a book for parents, 'What a Young Girl Ought to Know' is absolutely safe in the hands of a child. Its method of treating sexual questions in the same practical manner as, and together with, those of general personal hygiene and the development of character, to my mind enhances the value of the impressions concerning the sexual nature left with the young reader. It adds one more to the very limited list of books on this subject which can be unqualifiedly recommended for children's reading. As an incentive and aid to parental instruction it deserves the gratitude of all the mothers in the land; it is well equipped for its great mission."

MRS. ABBY MORTON DIAZ.
The well-known Author and Writer.

"Mothers will be thankful for so helpful a book. It presents in wonderfully well-chosen language—with illustrations from nature—a great deal they desire their girls to know, but can devise no good way of telling. A wide circulation of such books will work as a check to much of present evil. This whole matter of marriage and parentage and home training should form an advanced department of public education."

REV. WM. GOODELL FROST, Ph.D

President of Berea College.

"The little book, 'What a Young Girl Ought to Know,' is adapted to do incalculable good. Its aim and spirit are admirable, and it will be a practical demonstration to many of the possibility of treating the sanctities of our being in a worthy manner. Parents and teachers will find here suggestions which will give them the confidence in giving instructions which they have desired to impart, but been deterred from undertaking for lack of a model or precedent. Great is the power of the 'association of ideas.' It is simply horrible to have the most tender and sacred relations explained to our children by irresponsible and ignorant persons, and associated with all that is vulgar and vile."

PROF. C. P. COLER.
Instructor, Ann Arbor (Mich.) Bible Chairs.

"It is a much greater thing to save people from falling into sin than to rescue them after they have fallen I, therefore, regard your book, ' What a Young Girl Ought to Know,' as a very important contribution to Christian literature. Like Christianity, this book was born of love, and its words are warm with intelligent, maternal sympathy for all young girls. Dr. Mary Wood-Allen, the gifted author, is a devout Christian woman. She recognizes that there is a deep meaning in the words of her Master, 'Blessed are the pure in heart: for they shall see God.' I most earnestly commend the book to the careful consideration of parents, preachers, and teachers."

From **GRACE H. DODGE,**
THE PHILANTHROPIST.

"I have read with the deepest interest the little book published by you entitled 'What a Young Girl Ought to Know.' I want to thank you for issuing it and the companion books. They are just what are needed for many to use for the young people in their care. Dr. Mary Wood-Allen I have long known, and have myself learned great lessons from her. I know of no one who writes or speaks on these great subjects with more womanly touch, nor with deeper reverence. When I listen to her I feel that she has been inspired by a Higher Power. I trust many thousands of copies of the little book may go out with its great message, and know how it will help the young lives for whom it has been written."

From PROF. EARL BARNES,

FORMERLY PROFESSOR OF EDUCATION, LELAND STANFORD, JR., UNIVERSITY, CALIFORNIA.

"'What a Young Girl Ought to Know,' by Dr. Mary Wood-Allen and Sylvanus Stall, has just overtaken me here (London). I have read it with a great deal of interest, and I find it in no way inferior to the excellent work in similar lines which Dr. Allen has done before; on the contrary, it is an advance. Parents must give this information to their children, and they will find this book invaluable in assisting them. It gives information enough and not too much, and it gives it in a clean, strong form that will prove a tonic to the girls who read it."

Pure Books on Avoided Subjects

Books for Men
By Sylvanus Stall, D.D.

"What a Young Boy Ought to Know."
"What a Young Man Ought to Know."
"What a Young Husband Ought to Know."
"What a Man of 45 Ought to Know."

Books for Women
*By Mrs. Mary Wood-Allen, M.D.,
And Mrs. Emma F. A. Drake, M.D.*

"What a Young Girl Ought to Know."
"What a Young Woman Ought to Know."
"What a Young Wife Ought to Know."
"What a Woman of 45 Ought to Know."

PRICE AND BINDING

The books are issued in uniform size and but one style of binding, and sell in America at $1, in Great Britian at 4s., net, per copy, post free, whether sold singly or in sets.

PUBLISHED BY

IN THE UNITED STATES
THE VIR PUBLISHING COMPANY
1134 Real Estate Trust Building Philadelphia

IN ENGLAND
THE VIR PUBLISHING COMPANY
7 Imperial Arcade, Ludgate Circus, London, E.C.

IN CANADA
WILLIAM BRIGGS
29-33 Richmond Street West Toronto, Ontario

MARY WOOD-ALLEN, M.D.

PRICE $1.00 NET
4s. NET

PURITY AND TRUTH

Self and Sex Series

WHAT A YOUNG GIRL OUGHT TO KNOW

BY

MRS. MARY WOOD-ALLEN, M.D.

National Superintendent of the Purity Department Woman's Christian Temperance Union; Author of "The Man Wonderful in the House Beautiful," "Marvels of Our Bodily Dwelling," "Child Confidence Rewarded," "Teaching Truth," "Almost a Man," "Almost a Woman."

PHILADELPHIA, PA.: 1134 REAL ESTATE TRUST BUILDING
THE VIR PUBLISHING COMPANY
LONDON: 7, IMPERIAL ARCADE, LUDGATE CIRCUS, E. C.

TORONTO: WM. BRIGGS, 33 RICHMOND STREET, WEST

Entered at Stationers' Hall, London, England

Protected by International copyright in Great Britain and **all her** colonies, and, under the provisions of the Berne Convention, **in** Belgium, France, Germany, Italy, Spain, Switzerland, Tunis, Hayti, Luxembourg, Monaco, Montenegro, and Norway

[PRINTED IN THE UNITED STATES]

Dedicated

TO

THE THOUSANDS OF GIRLS WHOSE HONEST INQUIRIES CONCERNING THE ORIGIN OF LIFE AND BEING DESERVE SUCH A TRUTHFUL, INTELLIGENT, AND SATISFACTORY ANSWER AS WILL SAVE THEM FROM IGNORANCE, ENABLE THEM TO AVOID VICE, AND DELIVER THEM FROM SOLITARY AND SOCIAL SINS.

CONTENTS.

	PAGE.
Preface	17
Introductory	23

TWILIGHT TALK I.

The Question of the Origin of Life.—Everybody at One Time a Baby.—Children Become Grown People and Parents in Their Turn.—Classes of Objects—Organic and Inorganic.—Inorganic do not Reproduce Themselves.—Organic Substances do Reproduce Themselves.—The Seeds of Plants Contain the Next Generation of Plants.—Wisdom of God in Enabling Us to Raise Plants as We Wish............. 27

TWILIGHT TALK II.

Plants Alive and Feed on the Soil.—Certainty that Plants will Reproduce Themselves.—How Important this Fact is to Man.—Man's Power in Choice of

What He Will Plant.—Man Learns by Experience to Cultivate Plants to Meet His Own Needs.—One Plan in all Forms of Organized Life.—Man Produces New Varieties of Plants by Use of the Laws of Reproduction.—Has Learned How to Produce Flowers of Whatever Color or Size He Wishes.—Same True of Fruits.—Man a Worker With God............................ 35

TWILIGHT TALK III.

"Consider the Lilies, How They Grow."—Study of Plants Called Botany.—First Thing a Plant Does is to Grow.—Feeds on Soil, Water, Air.—Second Thing Plant Does is to Reproduce Itself.—To do this it Produces a Flower and Then the Seed.—Names of Different Parts of Plants, Corolla, Calyx, Stamen, Ovary, etc.—The Functions of These Parts in Producing the New Plant.—Little Plant May be Called a Baby Plant.—The Pollen, the Father, the Ovary, the Mother and the Flower, the Family Home.—The Father and

Mother Nature Not Always in the Same Flower.—The Office of Bees, Insects, etc., in Fertilization............. 43

TWILIGHT TALK IV.

Man Not Put Into a Finished World.—The World a Wonder Ball of Treasures.—Man Discovering These Treasures and Using Them.—Life in Animal Forms.—Two Natures Here Also.—Fathers and Mothers.—Eggs are Seeds, and Seeds are Eggs.—How Fish Reproduce but Never Know Their Children. 50

TWILIGHT TALK V.

Millions of Fish Eggs Never Become Fish.—A Good Thing for Us.—Warm-blooded Animals.—How They Reproduce.—Bird Life Teaches Us Lessons of Love and Tenderness.—Mammals Also Reproduce from Eggs.—But the Young Kept Within the Mother's Body Till Able to Live Independently.—Human Being the Highest Type of Life.—Human Babies the Most Helpless, and this Develops Love and Parental

Tenderness.—Man Intended to be Ruler Over the World, and Must be Taught by Older Friends What He Needs to Know........................ 63

TWILIGHT TALK VI.

Question Where Babies Come From Answered.—From an Egg Also.—Ovary in the Mother's Body.—Eggs Therein.—How Developed Into the Child.—The Child a Part of Both Father and Mother.—Cannot Understand all the Mystery of Life........................ 73

TWILIGHT TALK VII.

God as Our Father, Pities His Children.—Likes to Give Them Pleasure.—Is Sorry When We do Wrong.—Wants to Comfort Us.—We Understand God Because We, Too, Can be Parents and Love and Care for Our Children. — Parenthood Developed Little by Little.—Birds Build Nests.—Man Makes a Home.—The Child a Part of the Parent, and Bears a Record of Parents' Life, Thought and Conduct... 83

TWILIGHT TALK VIII.

Heredity.—What Our Ancestors Have Given Us.—This May be Physical, Mental or Moral.—The Children of To-Day, Making the Characters of the Children of the Future.—If All Children Were Good Now, the Men and Women of the Future Would be Good.—The Child Should be What He Wants His Children to Be.—What the World Would be Like if God Created Every Individual as He Did Adam and Eve.. 91

TWILIGHT TALK IX.

Value of Public Health.—Preventable Diseases.—Care of the Body.—Self-Abuse.—Its Penalties.—Girls Should Receive Their Instruction From Mother.—The Body a Temple to be Kept Pure and Holy.................. 101

TWILIGHT TALK X.

Why We Should Think Highly of Ourselves.—You are a Daughter of the King of Kings.—You are Not Your Body.—You are the Thinking Principle.—Your

Body, the Garment You Wear.—Body Made of Tiny Cells.—Every Act Destroys all Structure.—Why We Need to Bathe.—Water Needed in the System.—Objection to Tea and Coffee.—Influence of Girls on the Habits of Young Men.—Effects of Tobacco on the Body.—Freedom Very Desirable... 113

TWILIGHT TALK XI.

Effect of Thoughts.—Happy Thoughts Create Life-Forces.—Evil Thoughts Destroy.—Experiments Prove This.—Thoughts are Things.—You are Making in Your Childhood the Face You are to Wear When Old............... 129

TWILIGHT TALK XII.

Attitudes Affect Our Minds.—Tell How One Feels by How He Stands.—Walk denotes Character.—Wrong Postures Deform Both Body and Face.—Standing on One Leg Objectionable.—Sitting Stooped Over Produces Evil Results.—Rule for Correct Standing.—If the Children Stand and Walk Uprightly, the Men and Women in the Years to Come Will be Upright....... 137

TWILIGHT TALK XIII.

A Boy's Idea of the Value of Work.—Jesus Says, "My Father Worketh Hitherto, and I Work."—Work of Great Value in Self-Development.—Mr. Ruskin's Ideal of Women.—Mrs. Browning's Idea of the Value of Work.—Play Should be Recreation.—Play Should be Enjoyed in Proper Dress.—Everybody Should be Good Company for Himself.......................... 149

TWILIGHT TALK XIV.

The Value of Books as Good Company.—How to Judge Whether a Book is Good or Bad.—The Memory a Picture Gallery.—How We Store Away Pictures of Deeds, Acts, or Words, Not Only for Ourselves, but for Others.—Wise Choice of Book Friends Desirable.—What Shall We Read?.... 161

TWILIGHT TALK XV.

Friendships, Their Value.—Friendships Between Boys and Girls.—Girlish Intimacies.—Same Standard of Conduct for Both Sexes.—"Sowing Wild Oats."—Cannot be Too Choice in Companionship.—We are Souls Expressing Ourselves Through Bodies.—One Soul Lives in Man's Body, Another lives in Woman's Body, but Both are Souls.—The Influence of Young Girls.—Thoughts Weave Garments for Us..... 169

TWILIGHT TALK XVI.

What it is to Become a Woman.—The Bodily Changes at that Time.—Organs Not Fully Developed.—Should Have Time to Grow.—The Girl the Bud of the Woman.—New Mental Emotions to be Guarded.—Housework Good Exercise. 181

PREFACE.

There comes a time in the life of every intelligent girl when she begins to ask of her mother an explanation of the mystery of life's continued new manifestations. Her queries are not prompted by an unworthy curiosity, but are the outgrowth of a philosophic mental activity. The baby has no consciousness of self, does not even know that the little pink toes which she tries to put into her mouth are a part of her own organization. She learns through many experiences, painful and otherwise, of her existence. She realizes that she is one of many other existences. She observes that these existences are not stationary—they appear, they change, they disappear.

Plants start up through the soil; they develop, they wither and die. The birds come in the spring, build their nests, the little birds appear, grow up, and all pass out of sight with the approaching winter. Domestic animals come, in some mysterious way, into existence; and in an equally inexplicable manner their life may pass from them and leave them stiff and cold.

A new baby comes into the home or the neighborhood. A friend is sick, lies cold and still, and is laid away in the ground to reappear no more. Is it surprising that the thoughtful child observes these changes and wonders what they mean? Her little mind begins to wonder, "I am here. Was I always here?' Inquiry reveals the fact that there was a time in the life of her parents when she was not with them. Where was she then? She was not born. What is it to be born? Where is this invisible storehouse of life, from which is drawn the tiny helpless creature that has come to claim its place in the home-love and care?

Everybody, they say, was once a baby; then all must have come in the same fashion into earthly life. Did they come from the sky? And why does their coming always happen at the inopportune time when mother is ill? What is this strange, mysterious advent of life concerning which people are so silent?

Can you wonder that the intelligent, observing child begins to propound these queries? And if they are the result of observation of processes which cannot be kept hidden from the child, is not that, in itself, an indication that the truthful explanation is not to be withheld? We say these things are sacred, and yet the embarrassed manner with which we meet the child's inquiries is proof of some feeling of shame which should not be attached to a sacred theme. If we can bring our thoughts into harmony with God's plans, we shall find that pure instruction may be given in a way that will not only not contaminate the child's thought, but will be a safeguard during future life.

"But," says one mother, "I want to keep my daughter innocent as long as I can." And I reply, I go still further in my desires. I wish to keep them innocent always. But ignorance and innocence are not synonymous. Many children are deplorably ignorant who are far from innocent, while others may have much pure knowledge and be most sweetly innocent.

Myriads of mothers believe this in a general way, but do not know how to apply it to real life. They say, "I could not tell my sweet, pure child these facts of nature in language choice enough to insure that her thought should not be tainted. Tell me just what words to use."

This statement, which has been made over and over again to those who have been trying to lead the thought of mothers in this line, has called forth this little book. It hopes to solve much of the problem of the mother by showing her how the physiological facts of reproduction may be clothed in delicate language and surrounded by an atmosphere of sacredness and self-reverence that will render the knowledge thus obtained a guarantee of right conduct. The knowledge given is intended to meet every need until the girl is old enough to have the next book of the series placed in her hands.

It is thought wise to put the information suited to different ages in different volumes so that the girl will find what meets her present need and not be led into fields of investigation wider than the immediate case demands.

The plan laid down in this book is not a theory merely. It has been made a working hypothesis by so many in the past that it has gone beyond the realm of plausibility into that of certainty. We do not simply believe that it may be a good thing to forestall evil knowledge by wise, parental instruction, but we know that a pure knowledge is a most sure and trustworthy safeguard of present innocence and a reliable prophecy of future virtue.

MARY WOOD-ALLEN.
Ann Arbor, Mich.

SYLVANUS STALL.
Philadelphia, Pa.

INTRODUCTORY.

For the first time in her life Nina had been away from home without her father or mother. She had been visiting her Aunt Mary for two weeks and now her father had come to take her home. Very glad indeed was she to go home again to the dear mother and with great joy she saw the familiar places. "Oh, there is the school-house!" she exclaimed. "There is the crooked apple-tree! And there is home! But mother is not at the door. I thought she would be waiting for us."

"Your dear mother will be glad to see you," said her father, "but she is in her room. She has something to show you."

With rapid footsteps Nina sprang up

the stairs to her mother's room and was much surprised to find her mother lying in bed, pale, but looking very happy. "Are you sick, mother?" cried Nina.

"I am better," said the mother, smiling, "and I have something to show you."

Opening the blankets of a little bundle by her side, she showed the face of a baby.

"Oh!" exclaimed Nina, "a baby! Whose is it?"

"It is ours," said the mother, "your baby brother."

"Oh, where did it come from?" said the little girl. "Who brought it? Why didn't they bring a pretty one?"

The mother laughed as she said, "I think it is beautiful. I think there never was a baby so beautiful except one and that yourself."

"Did I look like that?" said Nina.

"Yes," said the mother, "very much. But this will grow more beautiful as time goes on."

"But tell me where it came from. Is it ours to keep?"

"Yes, it is ours to keep, and in a few weeks when I am stronger and better able to talk I will tell you where it came from. But you must remember this, my daughter, that the little one belongs to us, to you as well as to father and mother, and that you are to care for it and love it."

"But you will love me just the same," said Nina, "it will not take my place?"

"Oh no," said the mother, "never. It can never take the place of my little daughter in my heart. Now go and play, and just as soon as I am strong enough we will have our twilight talks again."

Ever since Nina could remember, it had been their custom to hold twilight talks. At the time of the children's hour Mrs. Grant, taking Nina close to her, would talk to her of all the sweet and beautiful things of life, and this twilight hour had become very precious both to the mother and the little girl. So, when a few weeks later, Mrs. Grant was strong enough and took Nina in the dying hours of the day to talk to her, it seemed very sweet and pleasant. Drawing close to her mother, Nina lay her head upon her shoulder and the first talk began.

TWILIGHT TALK I.

The Question of the Origin of Life.—Everybody at One Time a Baby.—Children Become Grown People and Parents in Their Turn.—Classes of Objects—Organic and Inorganic.—Inorganic do not Reproduce Themselves.—Organic Substances do Reproduce Themselves.—The Seeds of Plants Contain the Next Generation of Plants.—Wisdom of God in Enabling Us to Raise Plants as We Wish.

WHAT A YOUNG GIRL OUGHT TO KNOW.

TWILIGHT TALK I.

"It seems very pleasant, my daughter, to have our twilight hour together once more and the question you have asked is a very important one: 'How do people come into the world?' A few weeks ago the baby brother was not here, now he is here and we hope will stay with us until he is a grown man. All who are now living were once babies, just as small and helpless and sweet as he is. They grew up and to many of them have come little children, who will also grow up to be men and women, and in their turn become fathers and mothers. And so it has been, ever since the first man and woman lived on earth.

"We have in the Bible an account of the creation of Adam and Eve, the first man and woman, but since they were created we have no account of God's following that same plan in calling other human beings into life. We read that children came into the world and now you want to know what plan God did choose by means of which human life could be continued on the earth.

"As we study the world we find two classes of objects, one called the inorganic and the other organic. Inorganic objects are those which have no organs, no separate parts to do special work. Rocks, stones, earth, iron, gold, all the metals, are inorganic. They have no hands, feet, eyes or ears. They do not eat food and make it over into themselves. If they grow it is by material just like themselves being added to them from the outside. They cannot walk or make any kind of noise. They do not have life.

"Organic objects have life, and they are

made up of various parts or organs, each with its own work to do. All plants are organic, they are alive, they grow, they eat food from the soil and make it over into themselves. The little roots of the plant go down into the ground, take up water and various inorganic substances, and pass them on through the sap to the stem and leaves, which take these substances and make them over into themselves, so they are continually growing.

"It is very wonderful that the plant or tree can make the inorganic substance over into its own substance and always do its work the same way. The oak and the elm grow side by side in the same soil, and yet the sap in the oak carries material that is made always into the oak leaf, the oak fibre, and the acorn. It never makes a mistake and patterns after the elm. The grass which grows under the tree is fed by the same soil, but it differs from the trees, and also from the violets that hide under the leaves, or from the little anenome that peeps up so bravely in the spring. Why is it that each plant repeats itself each year? In the first chapter of Genesis we find the statement that this was God's intention, for it says in the eleventh and twelfth verses, 'And God said, Let the earth bring forth the grass, the herb yielding seed and the fruit trees yielding fruit after its kind whose seed is in itself upon the earth, and it was so, and the earth brought forth grass and herb, yielding seed after his kind and the trees yielding fruit whose seed was in itself after his kind; and God saw that it was good.'

"This is the law and the plants always obey it. Here is a tiny black speck that you say is grass seed and you are perfectly sure that if put into the ground, it will bring forth grass and never anything else. Its seed is in itself. Was it not very good of our heavenly Father to wrap up the life of the plant in the little seed and so put into our hands the power to produce plants where we want them? We can raise flowers, fruits or vegetables, because the plant can produce itself through the **seed**. And **we can** plant just **such** seeds **as we** want and **raise** the kind of plant that **we wish. This power of the** plant **to produce itself** again from the seed we call **reproductive power** and by it we are able to make **the** world into gardens, farms or **parks at** our pleasure."

TWILIGHT TALK II.

Plants Alive and Feed on the Soil.—Certainty that Plants will Reproduce Themselves.—How Important this Fact is to Man.—Man's Power in Choice of What He Will Plant.—Man Learns by Experience to Cultivate Plants to Meet His Own Needs.—One Plan in all Forms of Organized Life.—Man Produces New Varieties of Plants by Use of the Laws of Reproduction.—Has Learned How to Produce Flowers of Whatever Color or Size He Wishes.—Same True of Fruits.—Man a Worker With God.

TWILIGHT TALK II.

We talked last evening of how plants grow and reproduce themselves. Now when you put a seed into the ground you will be interested in thinking that it is alive, that it will take up food from the soil and begin to grow. Some of the food it will make into stem, and some into fruit, and in the fruit will be the seed which contains the life of the new plant. But the new plant, you remember, will always be like the parent plant. If that were not so there would be great trouble. The farmer would not know what harvest to expect from the seeds he puts into the ground. Now, he goes out into the field and sows wheat or oats, or plants corn or potatoes, knowing surely that his crop will be of that which he has planted. And if something unexpected does come up, it is because he made a mistake in the seed, for the seed never makes a mistake, it is true to its kind. Suppose that one oak tree were a strong kind of wood, as it is, and suited for ship building, and the next oak tree were brittle and a ship were made of it, you see that it would not stand the strain and so great loss of life and property might follow. But because the seed is always true to its kind, we know that the acorn will bring forth a tree with tough strong fibre, that may be safely built into ships on which we may trust ourselves to cross the ocean even in fierce storms. Men learn of the characteristics of one tree and then they always find that a tree of that kind will have the same characteristics. We can trust God. He keeps his promises with us and when he says the plant will bring forth after his kind we may be sure it will do so.

And so man wherever he goes can have his choice of food and flowers and shade trees among those suited to the climate where he lives. You see, God is not like a tyrant who says every one must do everything just a certain way, but like a kind parent who lets his children help him because it is good for them to work, not because he needs their help. You know that mother often lets you help her in arranging the rooms, because she thinks it is good for you to learn how to sweep and dust and place the furniture. It cultivates not only your hands, but your mind as well. You remember when I allowed you to have your own room arranged to please yourself. It was not done as I should have done it, and after a time you found that it might be arranged differently and suit you better. You learned more by the experience than you would if I had made you put things at first as you afterwards decided yourself to put them. So God allows us to plan and study and work and find out many things for ourselves. We are learning by experience how to cultivate plants and improve them. We are finding out the laws that govern them and making use of these laws to our own advantage. We are learning to think God's thoughts after him, and to understand why he has chosen certain plans.

In the study of reproduction in plants we are prepared for the study of reproduction of other organized beings, for God has made one plan that, with some changes, we find in all forms of organized life. We shall see, as we study, that God has shared his highest power with human beings.

It is very wonderful to see how man has learned to use the laws of reproduction in creating new varieties of plants. Men have studied this subject until they know how to produce double flowers from single ones, or a variety of colors from a plant of one color. I read the other day that from one little, yellow, single, Scotch rose there was produced in forty years over three hundred varieties of roses, differing in size, shape and color. Some of them were large and double. All colors were represented, from palest tint of pink and yellow to blush, and crimson and variegated.

Up to 1810 there were no varieties of pansies, but by 1835 four hundred varieties had been produced by selection and cultivation. It seems to me that we can almost say that creative power has been given to man when he, from a plant bearing only one form of flower, can produce so many varied forms of the same flower.

In the same way man has learned to produce different varieties of fruits. The original apple was the wild crab apple, small, sour and gnarly, but from this unpleasant little apple has been produced all the delicious apples of our orchards. When we see the beautiful garden flowers and taste the luscious orchard fruits, we may exclaim, "Behold, what hath God wrought!" and may also truthfully add, "See what hath man produced!"

TWILIGHT TALK III.

"Consider the Lilies, How They Grow."—Study of Plants Called Botany.—First Thing a Plant Does is to Grow.—Feeds on Soil, Water, Air.—Second Thing Plant Does is to Reproduce Itself.—To do this it Produces a Flower and Then the Seed.—Names of Different Parts of Plants, Corolla, Calyx, Stamen, Ovary, etc.—The Functions of These Parts in Producing the New Plant.—Little Plant May be Called a Baby Plant.—The Pollen, the Father, the Ovary, the Mother and the Flower, the Family Home.—The Father and Mother Nature Not Always in the Same Flower.—The Office of Bees, Insects, etc., in Fertilization.

TWILIGHT TALK III.

Having learned something of the wonders that man has produced in the plant world, you will want to know how he has been able to do this. First we will have to learn how plants reproduce themselves. I found something to-day in Gray's little book, "How Plants Grow," that I think will be a very good text for our talk. He quotes the verse, "Consider the lilies of the field how they grow. They toil not, neither do they spin, and yet I say unto you that even Solomon in all his glory was not arrayed like one of these." Then he says, "Our Lord's direct object from this lesson of the lilies was to convince the people of God's care for them. Now this clothing of the earth with plants and flowers, at once so beautiful and useful, so essential to all animal life, is one of the very ways in which he takes care of his creatures. And when Christ himself directs us to consider with attention the plants around us, to notice how they grow, how varied, how numerous, and how elegant they are, and with what exquisite skill they are fashioned and adorned, we shall surely find it profitable and pleasant to learn the lesson they teach."

If you were studying plants in school it would be called studying botany, but we will not try to learn all the hard names, but get hold of the facts in an easy way.

You remember that plants are organic. Their organs are the root, stem and leaves which are needed for growth and are called organs of vegetation. The flowers, fruit and seed are called the organs of reproduction. You understand that reproduction means, to produce or make again. So the organs of reproduction in plants are the organs through which they produce other plants like themselves. The first thing a plant must do is to grow, so the root takes food from the soil and the water, and the leaves also take food from the air, and in this way the plant grows. After a while it sets about reproducing itself, and the first thing it does is to produce a flower. Some plants blossom in a few weeks after springing from the seed, some do not blossom before the second summer and others have to grow several years before they bloom. Flowers are very beautiful to look at and have many shapes, colors and odors, but they are all intent on one object, and that is to produce the seed, in which is the life of the plant.

You may as well learn some of the names of the different parts of the flowers, so I will tell you that the beautiful tinted leaves of the flower all together are called the corolla, which means a little crown. When you see the morning-glory you will see that it wears a pink or purple crown. If you pull the crown off you will see five little green leaves, which held it, and these are the calyx, meaning cup. If we open the corolla we shall find five little stems, stamens they are called, growing fast to it. At the top of each stamen is a little hollow case and if we open it we will find it filled with a yellow powder, which is called the pollen. Now let us remember that the stamen with its little case of pollen is one part of the plant's organs of reproduction. The other part we find is left in the calyx. It is a long, slender, green stem rising from an enlarged portion, called the ovary, which is the vessel containing the seeds. At the top of the slender stem is a roughish enlargement, which is moist and is called the stigma. The stem is hollow and leads down into the ovary. If we cut through the ovary we will find it to contain the young seeds. The number of seeds differs in different plants. In the morning-glory there are only six. They are small, hard and black when they are ripe, and when put into the ground they begin to take up moisture and then begin to grow. But they will not grow unless they are fertilized. Some of the pollen must pass down into the ovary and reach the seeds, causing them to develop the principle of life. We do not know just exactly how this is done, but we have learned that if the pollen does not enter the ovary and fertilize the seeds, they will not grow. We see then that there is a union of something that is formed by one part of the plant and something that is created by another part of the plant, and life is the result.

We call the little new plant a baby-plant, so it will not be amiss to say that the pollen is the father and the ovary the mother, and the flower the home of the morning-glory family.

In all plants we find the same principle of reproduction, but we do not always find the two natures of the plant united in the one flower as we do in the morning-glory. In some plants the pollen is in one flower and the ovary in another;

or the flowers that bear the pollen may be all on one plant and the ovaries all on another plant. When they are found together in one plant, the pollen, or flower-dust, from the male anther is easily conveyed to the female stigma and thus passes down the style to the seeds and give them life.

When the pollen-bearing flower is entirely separate from the seed-bearing flower it is called imperfect, because neither flower alone can produce the fruit or seed. The Indian corn is of this kind. The tassels are the stamens and the "silk" that comes out of the husks is the style. The pollen from the "tassels" falls on the "silks" and is carried by each separate thread to each kernel of corn and gives it life. These kernels are the seeds of the new plant, but without the pollen they could never grow, even if planted in the ground. But sometimes the flower-family are still more widely separated and the pollen-flowers are on an entirely different shrub or tree from the seed-bearing flowers. They may even be miles apart and although each tree will bear flowers, there will be no fruit or seeds unless the pollen can come to visit the seed; and the wind and bees or other insects do good service in this respect. The busy bee intent on getting honey for himself has no idea that he is bearing life on his hairy thighs, but they are covered with the pollen he has caught in his visit to a flower and this will be left in the seed-bearing blossom of the same species of flower that he next chances to call upon. You remember the little verses,

"How doth the busy little bee
  Improve each shining hour,
And gathers honey all the day
  From every opening flower."

We might add to it another rhyme:

And while the little busy bee
  Gathers of sweets a store,
He carries life from flower to flower
  That they may yield him more.

I read a little poem to-day which pleased me and I learned it so that I might teach it to you. It was written by Emma L. McCord. You see she speaks of the flower as the nurse of the baby seeds. The poem is called

A BOTANY LESSON.

There's a strange wee cradle in each little flower,
    Where the wee seed-children are sleeping.
Though so small, they are growing hour by hour,
    And the nurse-flower watch is keeping.

All around and about are the stamen-trees,
    Where the gold pollen-cakes are growing,
And the bees and the butterflies shake the trees,
    And the little seeds think it is snowing.

But the snow, in flowerland, is yellow snow,
  And the sleepy little seed-flowers love it,
So each one eats (and this makes him grow),
  As the nurse-flower smiles above it.

When the little flower seeds look brown and dead,
  And the cradle becomes too small,
The nurse-flower, sleepily, nods her head,
  And among the leaves she drops them all,
  The sleepy little seed-children!

TWILIGHT TALK IV.

Man Not Put Into a Finished World.—The World a Wonder Ball of Treasures.—Man Discovering These Treasures and Using Them.—Life in Animal Forms.—Two Natures Here Also.—Fathers and Mothers.—Eggs are Seeds, and Seeds are Eggs.—How Fish Reproduce but Never Know Their Children.

TWILIGHT TALK IV.

We have found in our study of God's law of plant reproduction, that instead of making each separate plant by itself, He has provided a way by which all plants may continue the life of their kind on the earth. By so doing, He has given great power into the hand of man. God did not put man into a world that was all finished, where he would have nothing to do but to look about him to see wonderful things in which he had no part. But God put him into a great workshop full of all kinds of things to work with, and then he gave man skill to use the material in making the world to suit himself.

Man's brain and hands are the tools God gave him to work with and then it would seem that He left him to see what he could do with all these wonderful things. I have read that the Germans often give to their friends at Christmas time what they call a "Wonder Ball." This is a big ball of yarn and the one who receives it must knit something with the yarn, and as she knits she begins to find gifts hidden away in the ball. One after another they come into view as the yarn is used and when the whole ball is thus unwound there is some useful article and a number of gifts.

It seems to me that the earth is a great Wonder Ball which has been put into the hands of man. It is full of treasures of gold and silver and gas and oil, and out of these he is making many useful things. He is building cities, making railroads and ships, digging canals and tunneling mountains. He is discovering natural laws and using them for his own service. He makes electricity carry him from place to place, run on his errands, cook his food, light his house, print his books and sing songs for his entertainment.

He has found out how to see through boards and even into the body itself. He has learned not only to take pictures of what we can see, but to photograph our very thoughts. But the most wonderful power over which he has control is over this principle of life, by means of which he changes the waste places into gardens and makes the desert to blossom as a rose.

But let us study life in other forms. Plants have life, they grow, they reproduce, but they do not feel, they can not walk about. There is, then, a higher form of life than that which is found in plants, and that is animal life. I should like to tell you all about life in its varied forms, but when you are older you will study it. Just now I will tell you of the live creatures with which you are somewhat acquainted.

We found that in plants there were two natures, which must unite to create the new plant, and this is also the law of animal life. All animals are divided into male and female, that is, fathers and mothers. We learn that the animal mother has an ovary, just as the plant mother has; but instead of seeds it contains eggs.

We might call the seed of the plants their eggs, or we might call the eggs of the animal its seeds. It all means the same thing. The seed is that from which the baby plant will come and the egg is that from which the baby animal will come.

Do you know that serpents and fish have eggs? You remember that we have sometimes had what was called fish "roe" for dinner. The roe was merely the eggs of the female fish, probably a shad. The shad live in deep sea-water most of the year, but in the spring, when their bodies are full of eggs, they swim into the bay, or may be hundreds of miles up the river, to find a quiet place where they may lay their eggs.

The male fish go with the female fish on this journey and when they have found the place they are seeking, each female fish expels the eggs from her body and they float in the water. Their work is done, but the eggs will never become little fish unless they are fertilized, just as the seed never will become a plant unless it is fertilized. So the male fish swims over the eggs, and expels from his body a fluid which looks like the white of an egg. This fluid contains the principle of life, which entering into the eggs makes it possible for them to develop into the baby fish.

But they never know anything about their father and mother, who go away and never see, or at least never know their children. The eggs remain in the warm water, and in a few days are hatched and begin to live their own independent life.

TWILIGHT TALK V.

Millions of Fish Eggs Never Become Fish.—A Good Thing for Us.—Warm-blooded Animals.—How They Reproduce.—Bird Life Teaches Us Lessons of Love and Tenderness.—Mammals Also Reproduce from Eggs.—But the Young Kept Within the Mother's Body Till Able to Live Independently.—Human Being the Highest Type of Life.—Human Babies the Most Helpless, and this Develops Love and Parental Tenderness.—Man Intended to be Ruler Over the World, and Must be Taught by Older Friends What He Needs to Know.

TWILIGHT TALK V.

You feel very sorry for the little baby fish that are orphaned before they are born, and indeed they need your sympathy. Many of the eggs will be destroyed before they are hatched, and many of the little baby fish will be eaten up by other fish or various water animals, and so a very small number of the fish will grow to maturity. This is a good thing for us, for one fish lays thousands, or even millions of eggs, and if all developed into fish, they would fill the rivers so full of active fish life that it would be a very serious thing.

Frogs, serpents, fish and other creatures of this kind are called cold-blooded animals. But we will now talk of some of the warm-blooded animals which lay eggs. Of these the best known to you are the birds and the chickens. You remember last summer how interested we were in watching a pair of Baltimore orioles as they swung their nest from an elm tree near the house. We saw there were two birds building the nest, and after it was made one of them laid eggs and then sat down upon them to keep them warm. The other bird flew about, bringing her worms and other food, singing to her and keeping her company. And sometimes she would leave the nest and he would sit upon the eggs to keep them warm, for you see the one was the mother bird and the other the father bird. And after a time the little birds appeared in the nest and then the parents took care of them and fed them. They were better parents than the fish, and the birds were better children, for they stayed close to the mother and father, until they were taught how to fly, but then they flew away and the parents knew them no more.

The eggs of the bird were developed in the mother bird's body in an ovary. But these eggs might have been sat upon for weeks and months and no little birds have come into life, had not the eggs, while yet in the body of the mother been fertilized by a product from the male bird. Thus fertilized, the new life was given to them and when they were afterwards kept warm for three weeks, they developed into the little birds which gave you so much pleasure.

We learned many lessons of patience, love and tenderness in watching the birds and their nest-building. Now when we hear the birds singing and see the nest, we like to think of them as little bird-homes, wherein the father and mother and their children live, and we realize that in another form the birds are only repeating the life of the flowers.

Now we come to still higher forms of warm-blooded animals, those that feed their young from their own body. You know some of these, as the cat, dog, horse and cow. We find in each case that the baby animal is nourished by milk, which is produced in the body of the mother. You have seen the little kitten taking the food from the mother or the little calves from the cow, and know that this is the way in which these animals nourish their young. Therefore, they are called mammals, the word "mammal" being the same in its origin as "mamma," and meaning breast, the young being nourished from the mother's breast.

If you should say that, in the case of these animals, life is not produced from an egg, as in the lower creatures, you would be mistaken. Life comes also from an egg in the mammal, but the egg is not large nor covered with a hard shell, nor does the mother keep it warm in a nest, as do the birds and chickens. But the little egg is held close in the mother's body. This egg is so small that it cannot be seen without the aid of a magnifying glass, and it will never develop into the new creature until it is fertilized by the male. It may pass into the world unobserved and be lost, but if it is fertilized, it then remains in the mother's body in the little sack or home prepared for it. Here it grows day after day, and week after week. The mother's blood nourishes it, her breathing purifies and cleanses it, and so it is fed and grows until the time has come for it to live its independent life, when it comes into the world, or is born, we say. And even then it is dependent upon the mother for its subsistence, finding in her breast its food, being nourished in helplessness many weeks and months before it is able to go alone.

After its teeth grow it is weaned, and then is entirely independent of the mother's nourishment, but still dependent in many instances upon her for care. However, in the lower mammals the young are self-helpful at once.

I used to wonder why it is that among the lower animals the young are so soon able to help themselves, to run about and be quite independent, while the human baby is so very helpless at first and grows so slowly into his independent life; but I have now come to see that it is a very wise and beautiful thought of God that has made the human being so helpless in his babyhood. The more valuable the creature, the more helpless is his infancy.

Fish, serpents, frogs and their kind are of no great value, so they do not need a parent's attention. But birds are higher in the scale of life; they receive some parental care as to feeding, but are soon quite independent. From the first, they eat the same food as their parents.

Mammals are a still higher form of life, and they are fed with milk from the mother's body and cannot digest the food suited to the full-grown animal, therefore, they must stay close to the mother, until they are able to digest such food as she eats. Then she weans them and gives them no further thought or care.

The human being is the highest type of life and here we find the most helpless baby. It cannot help itself at first, in the least. You notice that baby brother cannot raise his head, but he is now able to move his hands and feet a little and to turn his head from side to side. At first he could not do that. Pretty soon he will lift his head. After a time he will try to bear his weight on his feet and will jump about in mother's arms. After some months he will try to stand up, and when he is nearly a year old he will probably be able to walk.

See how long it will take him to learn that which the colt will know in a few hours. He will be several months old before his teeth will begin to come and he will not be given solid food for a year, and all this because he is so very precious that he must be very carefully protected and nourished. You see it takes more time to develop the complete human being than it does the animal. The baby is not complete at birth. He is here in his beautiful bodily home, but he has not become acquainted with it. Slowly he learns to know his various bodily organs, to understand the use of hands and feet, to develop his senses of sight, hearing, feeling, tasting and smelling. Slowly he learns to think, to reason, to judge, to act, and all this because his conduct is of more importance than that of the horse or dog, because what he does has in it what we call a moral quality, that is, it is either right or wrong.

God made man in His own image, to be ruler over the world, and he must be fitted for his great work. This is best done by putting him, a helpless baby, into the kind, loving, patient care of those older than himself, who have already learned, through experience, the very things he will have to learn, in order to become the useful man and be worthy of his place as a child of God.

TWILIGHT TALK VI.

Question Where Babies Come From Answered.—From an Egg Also.—Ovary in the Mother's Body.—Eggs Therein.—How Developed Into the Child.—The Child a Part of Both Father and Mother.—Cannot Understand all the Mystery of Life.

TWILIGHT TALK VI.

And now I have come to the answering of the question, "Where do the babies come from?"

I remember seeing the storks in the Old World. They are big birds with long legs, and they often make their nests on the roofs of houses, and the people will not drive them away because they say they bring the babies. But this is only a legend. We know it is not true. We know the story of life. We know that the human baby comes from an egg. Not an egg large and with a hard shell like the bird's egg, but one so small that you could not see it without a strong magnifying glass. And this egg comes from an ovary, just as does the flower seed, or the egg of the bird.

In the mother's body is the ovary, and in the ovary is the egg. This egg can leave the ovary and find its way out into the world and be lost and no one be the wiser, but when it has been fertilized it will remain in a little sac in the mother's body, where it will grow and grow for three-fourths of a year.

What a wonderful change from the tiny egg, smaller than the point of a pin, to the baby which often weighs eight or ten pounds. And this change takes place within the mother's body. Here it lies warm and safe from danger, and the mother knows it is there, and loves it before she has seen it.

You now understand that every human being was once a part of its mother. Her blood was carried to it and fed it, not as it will be fed by food after birth, but just as your blood feeds your body. The blood carries material to every part of the body and each organ selects that which it needs and builds it into itself. The unborn child cannot eat food to make blood for itself, but the mother eats and her food makes blood, and a part of this blood goes to the child and passes through its body and it finds there the material it needs to grow from the tiny speck to the well-developed baby.

Let me tell it to you as I told your older brother when he asked, "Mamma, how big was I when I was made?"

"When you were made," I said, "you were but a tiny speck, not so big as the point of a needle. You could not have been seen except with a microscope. You might think that if you were so small you would have been lost, and so you would, if the kind heavenly Father had not taken especial care of you. He knew how precious little babies are and so He has made this little room in the mother's body where they can be kept from all harm until they are big enough to live their own separate lives."

Brother was greatly interested and wanted to know if I knew he was there. Mothers do know, for the baby is alive and sometimes the mother feels the movements of the little hand or foot as it knocks on the wall of the room, and it seems as if the little one were trying to speak and say, "Mother, I am here." It always seemed so to me and I would reply, "Good morning, little one; mother loves you." Just so I used to speak to you, my daughter, and then I would try to think how you would look when I should see you.

Three-quarters of a year you lived in this little room, and you grew and grew every day and because I wanted you to be happy, I tried to be happy all the time, and I was careful to eat good food so that you might be strong, and I tried to be gentle, kind, patient, persevering, in fact, everything that I wanted you to be, for I knew that everything I did would help to make you what you were 'to be.

I told you that the mother's blood was carried to the baby and nourished it, and you may ask how that was done. You have seen me make dumplings. I took the dough and put the apple in and gathered the dough all up in one place and pinched it together. <u>You are much like a dumpling.</u> Your skin is folded around you like the dough around the apple and is gathered together in one place on the front of the body. We call it the navel or umbilicus. Before you were born the skin at this point was continued in a long cord, which was connected with mamma, and through it the blood was carried to you. When the time came for you to go out into the world to live apart from me, the door of your little room opened with much pain and suffering to me, and then you came into the world, or were born, as we say. Then the cord, or tube, that connected you to me was cut, and, healing up, formed the navel or the place where the skin of the whole body is gathered together. When you drew your first breath into your lungs, you cried, and then I knew you were alive; and I laughed, and said, "Is it a boy or a girl?" After you were washed and dressed they brought you to me and laid you on my arm and, for the first time, I saw the face of the little baby I had loved so long. And now you know why you were so dear to me; now you understand why the mother should love the child. It is a part of herself. But it is also a part of the father's very self. The human egg would not have grown into the child any more than the bird's egg would have grown into the bird, unless it had been fertilized, and this was the father's part.

The germ of life lay wrapped up in the egg, but it would never wake up unless it were touched by the power that only the father could give.

When it felt that touch it awoke and began to grow and at length came into the world a little soul in a human body, to live on earth for a number of years, and then to live forever in that other world. You can understand in part how wonderful is the relation of the father and the mother and why their children are so dear to them.

"They twain shall be one flesh," says the Bible, and truly they have become one in the child that in itself comprises a part of each parent. We cannot understand all of the mystery of life, but we can see that God has given us a wonderful gift in these powers which bind us to each other as parents and children.

TWILIGHT TALK VII.

God as Our Father, Pities His Children.—Likes to Give Them Pleasure.—Is Sorry When We do Wrong.—Wants to Comfort Us.—We Understand God Because We, Too, Can be Parents and Love and Care for Our Children. — Parenthood Developed Little by Little.—Birds Build Nests.—Man Makes a Home.—The Child a Part of the Parent, and Bears a Record of Parents' Life, Thought and Conduct.

TWILIGHT TALK VII.

In one of our talks I said man must be fitted to take his high place as a child of God. We use these words often without considering what they mean and yet I believe that God is very desirous of having us comprehend his relation to us as a Father. The other day I took my Bible and found in the fifth and sixth chapters of Matthew alone twelve places where Jesus speaks of God as Father, and his teachings are full of the fatherhood of God. But this would have no meaning to us if we knew nothing of what fatherhood is. When we read: "Like as a father pitieth his children, so the Lord pitieth them that fear him," we begin to think, "How does a father pity his children?" In the first place, fathers provide for their children, food, clothing and shelter, that they may not feel cold or hunger. Then, fathers like to give their children pleasure. They are sorry if the little folks are disappointed. If they are sick, the father will watch over them and in every way try to ease their pain. You know that you like your father to be sorry for you if you are unhappy. I can remember when you were a tiny little thing, if you were hurt, you would run to father to have him pet you and say "Oh!" a few times, and then you were all right again.

Is it not a beautiful thought that our Heavenly Father pities us when we are in sorrow or in trouble. He pities us when we do wrong. Once when I was a child I told my father something which he knew was not quite true and he looked at me so sorrowfully that I was surprised. I could not then understand it, but now I can. I see that he pitied me because I had been so foolishly naughty as to do that which I knew was wrong, and I often think how sorry God must feel for us when he sees us doing the things which he knows will give us cause to repent.

But God not only has pity toward us, but He wants to comfort us. So when we read, "Thus saith the Lord, as one whom his mother comforteth so will I comfort you," we begin to think of how mothers comfort their children. You know how you want to come to mother to have her fold you in her arms when you are in any trouble. There isn't another place in the world so full of comfort as mother's arms, is there?

But, you see, it is because we know what father-love and mother-love is that we begin to catch a glimpse of what God's love is when He calls himself our Father. If there were no fathers and mothers in the world, we would have no idea what these words mean. How could God make human beings understand Him unless He gave them the experience of being fathers and mothers?

It seems as if God had the purpose of

working out the thought of fatherhood and motherhood little by little. Among the plants we find fathers and mothers, but really they know nothing about it, they do not feel, they do not act, they just accept. In the lower animal there is voluntary action, but even here they know no affection, they give no care. A little higher up, as with the birds, we find a giving up of comfort to secure the life of the young. Although they are such active little creatures, the birds sit patiently for weeks on the eggs; and they also feed their little ones for a time. The mammals show more love, and care longer for their young. And in all these cases there are two parents.

Now we come to man, and here we find both fathers and mothers uniting more in the preparation for the coming of each little one, and caring for it more tenderly after it has come. They do not build a nest, but they make a home, and to the best of their ability they make it bright and beautiful. And when the little baby makes its appearance they love it as they have never loved any other living creature. It is a part of themselves. They gave it life, but that is not all, they gave to it its various capabilities.

Do you remember once when you became very angry and I corrected you, you said, "Well, did you never get angry when you were a child?" and I replied, "Yes, and that is why it is easier for you to get angry." You were thoughtful for a time and then you asked, "Mother, will it make it easy for my little girl to get angry if I do not control my temper now while I am little?" I was very much better pleased at that than if you had said, "Well, then I am not as much to blame for my quick temper as you are."

Many people excuse themselves for a bad temper or other fault on the ground that it is an inheritance and so make no effort to overcome it. We hear much of heredity in these days, and while it is a very big subject it is still possible for you to understand something about it and at our next hour we will talk of heredity.

TWILIGHT TALK VIII.

Heredity.—What Our Ancestors Have Given Us.—This May be Physical, Mental or Moral.—The Children of To-Day, Making the Characters of the Children of the Future.—If All Children Were Good Now, the Men and Women of the Future Would be Good. —The Child Should be What He Wants His Children to Be.—What the World Would be Like if God Created Every Individual as He Did Adam and Eve.

TWILIGHT TALK VIII.

In our study of plants we learned of the great power man has in producing changes in plants as he pleases. When we look at the beautiful Jacqueminot or delicate tea rose and admire their beauty as God's handiwork, we can also remember that they are a product of man's skill in the use of natural law. The wild sweetbriar rose is the form God gave us and man has produced all these other forms from this one. Man could never change it from a rose to a dahlia or any other kind of a flower, but he has learned how he can change it from a single to a double rose, or from pink to crimson, or from white to pink. Men are deeply interested in the improvement of plants and great sums of money have been spent in experiments along this line.

Man has learned how to improve

animals also. He knows how to obtain just the qualities he wants. If he wants speed he selects parents who both have that quality and it is marvelous to read what has been accomplished in the development of speed in the horse.

Bird-fanciers can produce birds of varying size, color or other trait, and when they have produced something unusual they ask very high prices for it.

I have just read an advertisement of Angora kittens offered at $25 apiece. This shows you how much money men are willing to give for pure blooded animals.

We have seen how much men can do in improving the plant and animal creation. Why cannot he apply the same idea to the improvement of the human race? You will wonder how this can be of any interest or importance to you, a little girl. And yet, you can see that if every little girl were to take care of herself and make of herself, the strongest, best and noblest woman possible, it would make a great difference in the individuals of the human race in a few years, and it would make an even greater difference in the characteristics of the children who are to come. Supposing that I had understood the value of myself to the world and had taken especial pains to keep myself well and strong, to take care of my mind and to always do the things I ought to have done, how much better it might have been for you and for little brother, who have inherited from me many of my characteristics.

When a man dies and leaves his property, or any part of it, to some one, that person is his heir and the property is an inheritance. But parents do not have to die to give inheritance to their children. You have inherited from me my quick temper, also your ability to learn easily. You have my hair and eyes. From your father you have received the shape of your head, your nose, forehead and the peculiar shape of your hands. From him you have your love of music and your persistence. You have said that you cannot understand why Bess and Nell do not like to practice their music lessons, while you enjoy it. I have heard your Grandma Grant tell how your father when a boy used to practice on an old accordion until everybody was woefully tired of hearing it. Learning the accordion was not of much account, but it was a fine thing for him to persevere, and he has passed on that quality to you, and you can thank him that he did "keep at things" when he was a child and so make a good trait of character for you to inherit.

It is a great thought, but even a little girl can comprehend it, that the children of to-day are making the world what it will be in one hundred years to come. The Bible says, "Even a child is known by his doings." And we are learning that the doings of the child will be known in after generations by the doings of his children.

We older people are trying very hard to make the world better, but the time when we could have done the best work was when we were young, even when we were little children. Supposing that all children from now on were to be good, obedient, truthful, honest, studious and industrious, you can readily see that the men and women of the future (who are only the children grown up) would have all those desirable qualities, and their children would receive them in a great degree as an inheritance. The surest way to reform the world is for every one to realize of how much value are the little children. And even the children can realize it to some extent.

Supposing you now begin to train yourself as if you were your own little girl. It will not be hard for you to decide what you want your daughter to be. I am sure you will want her to be obedient, polite and generous. So when you find yourself failing in any of these qualities you can take yourself in hand

and say to yourself, "Now, my dear, you are not the little girl I want. You must do better than this," and I am sure it will help you.

If I could have known when I was of your age the things I am telling you, I could, by training myself in all good qualities, have made it much easier for you to be all that I could wish you to be. But my chance to do that is gone. After you were born I could not give you any different inheritance. All I can do now is to help you overcome any inherited traits that may be undesirable. But in overcoming your faults you are creating a better inheritance for your children, and so you can see that you are of greater importance to the world now than you will be after you are as old as I am and your children are already in the world.

I have sometimes fancied what the world would be like if each human being were created as was Adam and Eve, directly by the great Creator himself.

There would be no fathers and mothers, no Aunt Marys to visit, no Uncle Johns to buy you toys and books and take you on little journeys. No dear grandma or grandpas, no birthdays, no weddings, no children going home on Thanksgivings or Christmas, no dear little baby brothers or sisters, no sweet pictures of the Infant Jesus and His mother, no lullaby cradle songs, no children's books or magazines, no toys, no games; oh! this would be a dreary world with only grown-up people in it, and they not related to each other. We feel sorry for the man or woman who must live alone and without friends or relatives; but what would it be if all the world were made up of grown-up men and women, each with no tie of kinship to any other one. Would it not be a lonely and a selfish place? David said of God that "He setteth the solitary in families." That is, He puts the lonely ones of earth together in homes, where they are happy because they belong to each other and love each other.

And the family means the father, mother and children.

Now when we read in the first chapter of Genesis, "Male and female created He them," we see that the happiness and comfort and beauty of the world is secured by this fact. And because this is so we ought to think very sacredly of ourselves and of our relations to each other.

I never like to hear children teased about being lovers and sweethearts, for it is jesting about that which in itself is holy and should be spoken of reverently. Children cannot be lovers and marry. They can be good friends and playmates, but not till they are grown up ought they to think of being lovers, and then it is the most sacred and beautiful thing in life, because it leads to the founding of the home into which will come the little children with their smiles and dimples and sweet mischievous ways.

TWILIGHT TALK IX.

Value of Public Health.—Preventable Diseases.—Care of **the** Body.—Self-Abuse.—Its Penalties.—Girls **Should** Receive **Their** Instruction From Mother.—**The** Body **a Temple to be Kept Pure and** Holy.

TWILIGHT TALK IX.

A great English statesman once said, "Public health is public wealth." Public health is made up of the health of individuals, and the health of the grown people is very much what the children in their care of themselves have made it. It is the little children of to-day who are deciding what will be the health and vigor of the nation of the years to come, so you see the study of physiology is of great importance. I have read that a hundred thousand people die every year because of diseases which might have been prevented. Now, what sort of diseases can be prevented by the persons themselves? We know that many diseases might be prevented through obedience to sanitary laws, and yet not every individual is responsible because he is sick. You remember when you made yourself sick by eating maple taffy and you learned then that you had some responsibility in regard to your health. You remember, too, when you took cold from wading in the water in disobedience to mother's instructions, and again you suffered because you did not take care of yourself.

It is quite necessary that we should learn in childhood the value of health, should study our bodies, for our bodies are the tools by means of which we get acquainted with the world. It is a very wonderful thing that we never see each other; we only see the houses in which we live, for these bodies of ours are wonderful houses, with windows, and doors, and rooms, as I have often told you. You also ought to understand the value of this bodily house, because you can only have one such house as long as you live in the world. You can not move out of it into another one, you can not give it away or sell it; and no matter how badly it gets out of repair, you must live in it as long as you stay in the world. So you will understand that you must take good care of your body, keep every organ in perfect repair, and never let any one else injure it.

You have only one pair of eyes and ought to take good care of them. I have seen persons reading by twilight, or by poor lamp-light, straining their eyes just as carelessly as though they could get a new pair as easily as they could buy a new pair of spectacles. You ought never to put your finger in your eyes, nor let any one else. Well, you say, you wouldn't do that; but I once knew a little girl who used to pull the corners of her eyes down and at the same time put her thumbs in her mouth and pull the corners of her mouth up, just to make other people laugh when they looked at her; and so she deformed her face and made it very ugly.

You would not put sticks or stones in

your ears nor let any one else do so. Every organ of the body is sacred and should be protected, and this is just as true of the sexual organs as of the eyes or ears. You should never handle them or allow any one else. And yet, girls sometimes form a habit of handling their sexual organs because they find a certain pleasure in so doing. Maybe they have never known that it is wrong, but usually they are ashamed of it, and as they go alone to practice this habit, it is called the habit of solitary vice. Perhaps they do not imagine that any one will know that they are guilty of this habit, because they are alone when they practice it, but it leaves its mark upon the face so that those who are wise may know what the girl is doing.

I was reading the other day what a certain wise physician has said about the effects of this habit. He is convinced that it causes a great many backaches and sideaches and other aches, tenderness of the spine, nervousness, indolence, pale cheeks, hollow eyes and languid manner. He says that we can almost always tell when a girl begins this habit of solitary vice, or self-abuse, as it is sometimes called, for she will suddenly decline in health and change in disposition. Instead of being happy, obliging, gentle and kind, she will very soon become peevish, irritable, morose and disobedient. She will lose her memory and love of study. She may become bold in her manner instead of being modest, as a little girl should be. She will be very indisposed to activity. She will manifest an unnatural appetite, sometimes desiring mustard, pepper, vinegar, and spices, cloves, clay, salt, chalk, charcoal, etc., which appetites certainly are not natural for little girls. Sometimes there is ulceration about the roots of the nails, and the eyes will look blank. This is a very serious penalty to pay for any pleasure that one may derive from this habit.

It is always easier to form a bad habit than to cure it, therefore, the best way to do is to form good habits in the first place. If a girl always thinks purely and sacredly of herself she will not be apt to fall into this vicious habit; if she remembers that every organ is sacred and its use ordained of God, she will not use it in such a way as to bring upon herself such serious difficulties.

There are certain organs of the body which we use openly in society; there are others which are to be used only in solitude, not because they are vile, but because it is refined and polite not to use them in public. We do not carry our garbage pail into the parlor, and yet we know it is just as important that the garbage pail should be emptied every day as that we shall have piano-playing, or even more, for the health of the family will depend upon the kitchen being kept clean. We do not entertain our friends in the laundry, where the soiled clothes are being cleansed, and yet we know that it is very important that the washing should be done, and we do not speak of it as something evil or vile, although it is not altogether pleasant.

So there are certain offices of various organs of the body which are performed by polite and delicate people only in solitude. We come together around the table to enjoy eating, in company with each other, and we know that this process of eating is for the building up of the body. The food which we take into the mouth passes into the stomach, is digested, and goes on into the bowels, where it is absorbed. It then goes into the blood and the various particles are taken up by the blood and passed on into the tissues, where they are made over into the substance of the body. But not everything that we eat is so used. A certain part of our food remains as waste and must be cast out of the body, just as the apple peelings and potato parings and things of this sort must be removed from the kitchen in order to keep things clean. It is very important that this bodily housekeeping shall be promptly and regularly attended to every day. It is a part of refinement and delicacy not to retain in the body these products of waste. We take fluids into the body in water, milk or fruit, and these fluids, passing through the system, wash it out and are then thrown out of the body in fluid form. It is very important that this duty shall be attended to promptly by the little girl, just as important as that mother shall attend to keeping the dwelling clean; but because the little girl desires to be ladylike and refined, she should do this when alone and not in company with others.

Children sometimes go with each other to the closet and often their talk is not what it should be. The little girl who values her modesty, who thinks highly of herself, will never allow anyone to talk to her concerning any part of her body in a way that is not sweet and pure, and if any child ventures to give her information concerning herself that seems to her such as she would not tell her mother, the wisest thing for her to do would be to say: "I would rather you would not tell me about it. I will ask my mother and she will tell me. Mother tells me everything that I ought to know and she tells it to me in such a way that makes it very sweet to me, and so I have my little secrets with mother, and not with other girls."

I do not think it is necessary to talk to you much about the evil habits which are formed, because I think you will remember always that your body is a beautiful house in which you dwell, and not only that, but that it is a sacred temple in which God dwells with you, and so you will always think of yourself so sweetly and purely that you will have no temptation to listen to evil words or to form evil habits. I would like to have you learn those words of St. Paul, "What! know ye not that your body is the temple of the Holy Ghost, which is in you, which ye have of God, and ye are not your own, for ye are bought with a price, therefore, glorify God in your spirit and in your body, which are God's."

TWILIGHT TALK X.

Why We Should Think Highly of Ourselves.—You are a Daughter of the King of Kings.—You are Not Your Body.—You are the Thinking Principle.—Your Body, the Garment You Wear.—Body Made of Tiny Cells.—Every Act Destroys all Structure.—Why We Need to Bathe.—Water Needed in the System.—Objection to Tea and Coffee.—Influence of Girls on the Habits of Young Men.—Effects of Tobacco on the Body.—Freedom Very Desirable.

TWILIGHT TALK X.

Paul called the body a temple. A temple, you know, is a place of worship, and it is the same as if he called the body a church. We know how sacred a church is to us. We feel that we must behave very properly when we are in church, but a church is made by man's hands, and the body is made by the hand of the great Creator and is, therefore, much more sacred than any church. So we ought to think of ourselves very highly, and with reverence, which means with love and affection. But you will say the Bible says we should not think of ourselves more highly than we ought to think. That is true, but there are different ways of thinking highly of ourselves. Some people think highly of themselves by imagining that they are very beautiful or very smart, and so try to show off and win praise. Another way of thinking highly is for people to regard their bodies as sacred and to reverence them because they are created by the Divine Power, and because we were of so much importance that Christ died for us.

You wear the little silver cross, which says that you are the daughter of a King. You would think that any earthly princess should wear beautiful clothes and be very beautiful in person, but you are the daughter of the King of kings and are beautifully clothed in the body, which is the garment God has made for you, for you are not your body. You are the thinking principle within, and the body is just the garment that you wear. It has been made so beautiful by the Divine Hand and it is cared for and kept in repair by Divine Power.

If we could see the body by a microscope or magnifying glass, we would see that it is made of very small atoms, called cells, and each one of these cells has a certain time to live. Our bodies are kept in repair by the food we eat. It is taken into the stomach and made over into a fluid, which is carried into the blood vessels and, becoming blood, is taken to every tissue in the body. From the blood the different tissues select that which they need, but there would be no room for new material if it were not that some of the material dies and must be carried out of the way. Every act of your life causes a change in the cells of the body, which tends to their destruction.

If all the activities of the body are destroying some part of its substance, what becomes of this dead material? It is being cast out through various organs of the body. Through the bowels a quantity of solid waste matter is cast out; through the bladder, fluid waste matter, and a large quantity of waste material passes out invisibly through the lungs and through the skin. You will be surprised to know that a larger amount passes out through the skin in twenty-four hours than through the bowels.

This shows the necessity of frequent bathing, for the surface of the body is covered with little pores or mouths and these need to be kept open in order that we shall be well. If the material which passes out is allowed to accumulate on the surface of the body it closes up these little mouths and people do not feel well. So you see the necessity of keeping the body clean. We clean our houses very frequently. We ought to clean our bodily dwellings very often also. We ought to keep the surface pure and we should eat only those things which go to build up the body, and not those which tend to fill it with dead material. Many children who are eating constantly of sweets and indigestible substances are sick, when they would have good health if they ate only simple, nourishing food, and ate that regularly.

It is just as important that the little girl should keep well as that the grown woman should keep well. She should learn in her early childhood to have that care of every part of the body which will keep it in perfect health.

In cleansing the body it becomes necessary to wash every part, and this is in accordance with refinement and delicacy; but, as I have said, no part should be handled for any other purpose. Sometimes when girls do not attend promptly to the daily movement of the bowels the matter collects in the lower bowel, and little worms gather there and then wander out of the bowels into the other private parts to create irritation. The girl may try to quiet this itching by her hands and so acquire the evil habit of solitary vice. But if she attends to eating simple food, to having the bowels move once a day, to keeping the private parts clean, she will not be troubled with this itching sensation, and so will have no temptation to allay it by the use of her hand.

I have spoken of wholesome food. I ought also to speak of wholesome drinks. Water is the only natural drink and pure water is the best fluid to take into the system. In fruits we take fluids in a very pleasant way, and milk is to a large extent water. From these three sources we will obtain as much water as is needed. Tea and coffee are very injurious, especially to children. They make people feel that they have had something to eat, when in reality they have given nothing to the nourishment of the body. They are both stimulants, and a stimulant is that which acts as a whip to create an appearance of strength, without really giving strength. Children need nourishing food to build up new material as well as to keep the body in repair, and if they take into the body that which makes them feel as if they have been fed, when they have not been fed, it is very injurious. I always feel sorry when I see young people using tea and coffee.

Perhaps you remember your little cousin Willie, who at ten years of age used to have sick headaches if he did not have his cup of strong coffee for breakfast. His mother did not realize that it was the coffee that injured him, and that the sick headache was caused by the nerves demanding the stimulant to which they had become accustomed. I am sure my little daughter will be well satisfied with water and milk, and not desire to take into her system something which is poisonous and injurious. If she does not begin the use of tea or coffee when a little girl, in all probability she will never take up their use later in life, which will be greatly to her advantage. It is unwise for us in our younger days to create false necessities. Sometimes when I have been traveling I have seen people, who, because they could not get a cup of tea or coffee, were having the headache and feeeling very uncomfortable, while I, who drink neither, was perfectly satisfied with my cold lunch and cup of cold water. I had had food and drink, and while I would have enjoyed a warm meal, it was not a necessity either to my health or happiness. When we really think about it, it seems very small to be a slave to such little things. It is far nobler to master the body than to be mastered by it, and that girl is wise who will not allow herself to form a habit that will make her in any degree a slave.

Of course I do not need to talk to you about the use of alcoholic liquors, when you recognize them as such, but there are forms in which they may be offered to you, in which you will not recognize them. For example, cider, after it has been made a few days, begins to have alcohol in it, and so is objectionable. All wines contain alcohol. Homemade beer, if allowed to ferment, contains alcohol; so when these things are offered to you, you will be wise to refuse them because you do not wish to countenance in any sense the use of alcoholic liquors. Science is telling us every day of their injurious effect and we are beginning to learn that alcohol may be banished, not only from food and from social parties, but also from the medicine chest.

Girls have much responsibility, too, in regard to the use of alcoholic drinks by young men. Many young men have gone to drunkards' graves because they could not refuse the wine-glass when offered to them by some pretty, laughing girl, whom they greatly admired.

Girls also are largely responsible for the use of tobacco by young men, and, I am sorry to say, that girls themselves sometimes smoke cigarettes, thinking it funny; whereas if they really knew the poisonous effect of tobacco they certainly would not use it themselves, nor countenance its use in others. Boys get an idea that smoking is manly, but if they were made to feel that girls thought less of them when they smoke, it would have a great influence upon them, I am sure.

Even the little girl may have an opinion and by her expression of it when occasion requires may help some boy to give up tobacco. Of course, it would not be becoming for you to try to instruct older men, or take them to task for a bad habit, but if one should ask your opinion, you ought to express it politely and have a scientific reason to give why you hold such an opinion. Therefore, I would like to have you study this question of the use of tobacco, so you will know just exactly why you object to its use. Tobacco is very injurious to the nerves. It paralyzes them, that is, it destroys their power, either their power of motion or their power of feeling. The man who uses tobacco, when under its influence does not realize that he is tired or ill, simply because the nerves that should tell him of his fatigue or illness have for the time being become paralyzed. Tobacco will affect his heart, making it beat too rapidly and so weaken it and shorten his life. It sometimes causes severe throat trouble. General Grant and Emperor Frederick both died with throat difficulty which physicians unite in believing were caused by the use of tobacco; and your own uncle died, when a young man, from a similar throat trouble from the use of tobacco. So I feel very strongly on this point and would like to have you have a very firmly fixed opinion and be ready to express it, for although you are only a young girl, you can understand these matters and your own responsibility.

Very many children die of infantile paralysis because the father is a tobacco-user, and many women are made invalids because their husbands use tobacco and the house is strongly scented with the odor of the poison it contains.

The heart of the grown person should beat about seventy-eight times a minute. A doctor told me the other day that he was called in to see a boy whose heart beat a hundred and forty times a minute and yet he had no fever. The doctor could not understand it until he discovered that the boy was a cigarette-smoker, and then it was all plain to him because he knew the effect of tobacco upon the heart.

School teachers tell us that boys who

use tobacco do not keep up with their classes at school as do those who do not use it. Remembering what I have said to you in regard to heredity, the transmission of the traits of parents to the children, you will understand that the use of tobacco by the boys of to-day is a very serious matter in regard to the future of the children in the years to come.

We often see notices put up in the vestibules of churches that tobacco must not be used in the church building, and we all think that is perfectly right, because the church is sacred; but no building erected by man can be so sacred as the temple of the body, created by the Heavenly Architect himself.

"But," you say, "a great many good men use tobacco, and they certainly would not use it if it were so hurtful." These men began the use of it probably in their youth, before science had told us much in regard to it. Now that they have formed the habit, they find it almost impossible to break it, and that, to my mind, is a very good reason for objecting to the use of all substances that enslave us. I was once a lover of tea, and after a time I became aware of the fact that I was becoming a slave to tea, and I didn't want to be a slave, I wanted to be free and so I gave it up, simply because I was not willing to come under the dominion of anything that was not an absolute necessity. I want you to grow up a free woman, free from all habits that are wrong, from everything that fetters and chains you. I want you to be free to think, free to act, and free to serve God with every faculty of your mind and body. I don't want you to use anything that will prevent your thinking clearly, or that will dull your judgment or your moral sense or make you in any degree less a perfect, noble woman than God designed you to be. As George Macdonald says, "I want to help you to grow as beautiful as God meant you to be, when He first thought of you."

TWILIGHT TALK XI.

Effect of Thoughts.—Happy Thoughts Create Life-Forces. — Evil Thoughts Destroy.—Experiments Prove This.—Thoughts are Things.—You are Making in Your Childhood the Face You are to Wear When Old.

TWILIGHT TALK XI.

I have told you how the body is either built up or destroyed by the substances which we take into the mouth, and now I want to tell you a little about how the body may be built up or destroyed by the thoughts which we hold in our minds. You know the Bible says, "As a man thinketh in his heart so is he," but we have only partly understood it. We have known that it was wrong to think evil thoughts, to indulge in evil passions or desires, but we have not known until lately how the thoughts and feelings of our hearts are really affecting our bodily condition. You know that if you are not happy you lose your appetite. You don't want to eat if you have had a very serious disappointment. If you get bad news just after you have had your dinner, it makes you feel very uncomfortable; the food will not digest. If you are very much afraid, your body will tremble and your face grow pale. If you are very happy, your body grows warm and your face grows rosy. If you are anxious, or dispirited, or worried in any way, the color of your face and its expression will show it, and this is all an intimation of how the thoughts of the mind are really creating the conditions of the body.

A few weeks ago I had the pleasure of talking an hour or two with a gentleman who has made this subject a great study. He took me into his laboratory and showed me a little instrument, by means of which he can detect the mental condition of a patient. He will have the person breathe into a glass tube. Then he will have the breath condensed by application of cold, subjected to the action of some chemical, and by the color which the chemical produces in the breath he will tell what the mental condition is. If it turns one color, he will know that the person is angry; if another color, he will know that the person is sorrowful; and if still another color, he will know that the person is remorseful for some wrong deed; and so he is able to detect the condition of the mind of the individual by the chemical analysis of his breath. By these experiments we can see that the thought in the mind really creates the condition of the body.

If it is true, as these experiments show, that evil thoughts create actual poisons in the blood, you will see how necessary it is for us to think only beautiful thoughts. How unwise it is for us to be impatient, or fretful, or angry, or jealous; to feel unkind or hateful feeling toward anyone else. It hurts ourselves worse than it can possibly hurt the other.

It is just as true that all kind and good thoughts create life-giving forces in our blood; so when we are happy, we are more alive, stronger, have better health than when unhappy or bad-tempered. When we are cheerful, contented, and serene, feel kindly towards everyone, we are doing the best for ourselves that we possibly can. So if we want to keep this temple of the body in good condition, we want to invite into it as guests, only the sweet and lovely thoughts which can truly be associated with God himself. He has promised to dwell in us and He cannot dwell in perfection where there are evil thoughts or evil feelings. Therefore we should remember that by the books we read or the pictures we look at, the thoughts we think or the words we say, we are creating the conditions of our own bodies, and if our thoughts are not pure, good and uplifting, we shall suffer in some bodily condition. We may quite truly say that thoughts are really things. They write themselves not only on the blood, but on tissues of the body. You can read anger, or sorrow, or irritability, or pleasure, and joy in the faces of the people whom you meet, because their thoughts write themselves there. We cannot afford to be irritable, or angry, because these feelings are making pathways in the brain for irritable or angry thoughts to come again and again, and they will write themselves on our faces until we look irritated or angry all the time.

You, as a little girl, are making the face you will have to wear when an old woman. Now, what kind of a face do you want when you are old? Just such a face as grandma's? Well, I am sure grandma would be pleased to hear that. She has had her sorrows and trials like other people, but she has never allowed them to make her feel bitter or angry, nor to express those feelings in her face, and now that she is old, she has a sweet, lovely expression that makes you wish to be like her. And you can be, but you will have to begin now as a little child to cultivate all those feelings which will express themselves with sweetness in your face. How can you do it?

Now I have a little secret to tell you, daughter. You can change your feelings by changing the expression of your face. Sometimes when you are angry, just make yourself look pleasant, smile, look as though you felt happy, and in a little while you will begin to feel the happy thoughts coming. You have created them by making yourself look as if you felt them, and so you can begin in your young girlhood to make of yourself, in your face and in your character, all that is true and noble.

TWILIGHT TALK XII.

Attitudes Affect Our Minds.—Tell How One Feels by How He Stands.—Walk denotes Character.—Wrong Postures Deform Both Body and Face.—Standing on One Leg Objectionable.—Sitting Stooped Over Produces Evil Results.—Rule for Correct Standing.—If the Children Stand and Walk Uprightly, the Men and Women in the Years to Come Will be Upright.

TWILIGHT TALK XII.

Last evening we talked of the effect of our thoughts upon the expression of our faces, and also of the expression of our faces upon our thoughts. I have now another little secret to tell you which is, that the attitude of our bodies has its effect upon our minds; and also that our thoughts and feelings affect our attitudes. You can judge pretty nearly how a man feels by how he stands.

Suppose we make a little experiment. Stand up right here before me. Let your knees bend a little; droop your shoulders forward, letting the arms hang loosely. Let the head be thrust forward, drop the chin, and open the mouth a little. There, how do you feel? I am sure you do not feel like doing any very wonderful thing. You are not wanting to run, or work; you could not start to climb Vesuvius, or run a race, as long as you keep that attitude. Now begin to think of climbing or running, or doing anything that takes strength, courage, activity. See how your knees stiffen, your back straightens, your head is lifted, your mouth closes, your eyes begin to shine, you feel courage, enthusiasm, a desire to act, and a feeling of power and belief that you can act. Now throw yourself here on the sofa, relax every muscle, let the limbs fall as they please. Now you feel lazily comfortable, you do not want to stir. Begin to think of going at once to ride, or row, or walk, and you cannot be still, your body begins to express the desire of your mind.

See the difference in the attitude of two boys, one of whom is laughingly teasing his companion. He is standing on one foot, his head bent forward and tipped to one side; the other stands firm on both feet, his head thrown back and both fists clinched. You can read their thoughts by their attitude.

Notice many people as they walk. One shambles along, dragging his heels and shuffling his feet. His whole body seeems loose and ungainly. You will not expect him to be a very prompt, energetic, thorough-going workman. Another steps briskly, cleanly. He does not scrape his feet on the walk. They come down firmly at every step with a clear, ringing sound. His body looks vigorous, energetic. You expect him to work with decision, to act with promptness. It would seem as if Solomon understood something of this matter, for he says. "The man of understanding walketh uprightly."

It is very important that children should learn to walk and stand properly. If that shambling man had been taught to walk as he ought when a child, it would have made him think differently; it would have changed his very character.

When I was a girl no one paid any attention to the matter of attitudes in sitting or standing, but now the learned doctors are thinking along these lines and are learning that many evils result from wrong postures. Dr. Eliza Mosher says that a flat chest is rarely seen in children when very young, but begins to show itself during school life, when they sit for hours in bent positions over their books. She says, too, that the habit of standing on one leg will not only cause the body to grow out of shape, but it causes the face to become one-sided, one side being rounded out and the other flattened. One side of the mouth will droop, the nose will incline to one side, and one eye will be open wider than the other. So you see if you want to have a pretty and symmetrical face it is important that you learn how to stand while you are a little girl.

But this is not all the evil that results from standing on one leg, she says. She thinks that fatigue of the eyes may be caused in this way. A very serious matter for young girls is that this position shortens one side of the body and crowds the internal organs out of place, and this may become a great source of trouble when later in life they may become wives and mothers. Dr. Mosher has made a very thorough study of postures of body and their results. Children, she says, should be taught to sit squarely erect, all twisting or drooping of the body should be avoided.

You remember how Miss Warren would not let you sit in school with one elbow on your desk, and you thought she was unkind, but she really was kind in this rule, for, like standing on one leg, it produces one-sidedness and all its evils for girls. You will understand that it really is more important that girls should grow straight than boys, for the girls, are to grow into women and in all probability become mothers, and the lives of themselves and their children may depend on the perfect symmetry of their bodies. Symmetry means being alike on both sides.

Sitting stooped over is productive of evil also, as it bends the body on itself and crowds the internal organs together. You know that the little baby must live for three-fourths of a year within its mother's body, and it must have room to grow; and if the mother did not grow straight as a girl, but grew twisted or one-sided, then perhaps the little room in which the child was to form and grow did not develop as it should, or it grew out of shape, and many troubles might follow. You will not need to know about the bad results if you take warning and keep yourself straight both in sitting and standing.

But how are you to know when you are sitting or standing as you should? I will give you Dr. Mosher's rule. She says: "Stand with your heels behind your belt line, draw your chin back to the neck with your head level, in this position relax your muscles; or place one foot half its length behind its fellow, and without changing the position of the upper part of the body, slide the other foot back until the heels are in line. When the body is to rest upon the feet, place one foot with the heel behind the belt line and the other a little in advance; make the knee of the posterior leg firm and rest the weight of the body upon it, relaxing the muscles of the other leg. Transfer the weight from one leg to the other without changing the position of the pelvis."

It is very important that you should learn to stand and sit as you ought, because of the effect that wrong postures have on the body, and it becomes more serious when we realize how postures affect the mind.

The children of to-day are forming the character and determining the destiny of the nation of the future, and they now, in their childhood, can decide what they want the nation to be and by their own lives secure it. If the children all grow up straight, the men and women will be straight. If the children think as well as walk uprightly, we shall have a race of upright men and women in the years to come.

You did not realize, did you, dear, of how much value the children are to the world, and how the world in hundreds of years to come will know just what the children of to-day have been?

You see, you are of more importance to-day than the grown people, for we have made our impress on the world through our children. You still have the chance to make of yourself what you please, and so do better things for your children than we did for ours.

Children sometimes blame their parents because of their failure to give to them a better inheritance, but that does no good. It is too late to change that, but there is still chance to improve themselves and so give their children a better start. We older people did not know as much about these things when we were young as you do now, so we are not as much to blame for our failure to give you good inheritances as you will be if you fail to give your children a good inheritance.

TWILIGHT TALK XIII.

A Boy's Idea of the Value of Work.—Jesus Says, "My Father Worketh Hitherto, and I Work."—Work of Great Value in Self-Development.—Mr. Ruskin's Ideal of Women.—Mrs. Browning's Idea of the Value of Work.—Play Should be Recreation.—Play Should be Enjoyed in Proper Dress.—Everybody Should be Good Company for Himself.

TWILIGHT TALK XIII.

When you were a little girl you were very fond of stories, and sometimes if you awakened in the middle of the night you would say, "Go on with your story," so I am going to begin this little talk with a story.

Once a little bare-foot boy was walking along the road with a tin pail in his hand. He met a very beautifully dressed girl about his own age. She stopped him and, rather commandingly, said, "Where are you going?"

"I am going to carry my father's dinner to him over at the mill," said the boy.

"Oh!" said the girl, disdainfully. "Then your father is a poor man and has to work?"

"Why, yes," said the boy, proudly, "my father has to work; doesn't yours?"

"Oh no, indeed!" said the little girl. "My father is rich and don't have to work." Then, looking at the boy pityingly, she said, "Just think what a dreadful thing it would be for the poor people if all the rich people should die!"

"Oh," said the little boy, "just think what a dreadful thing it would be for the rich people if all the poor people were to die! The rich people can eat good dinners, but they can't cook them; they can live in fine houses, but they can't build them. Oh, we poor people ought to feel very sorry for the rich, for it's hard to be like them."

Now I think this little boy had a far wiser idea of the value of work than the girl. It is strange how some people think it is belittling to work. I remember when I was a young woman at boarding school of hearing some girls trying to humiliate a new scholar whose hands were red and who looked as if she knew how to work. They were boasting of what they could not do, apparently thinking she would be ashamed of being a working girl.

"Why," said one of them, "I never did a stroke of work in my life."

"Didn't?" said the country girl. "Don't you know how to wash dishes?"

"Oh, no, indeed!"

"Can't you cook?"

"No."

"Wash, iron, bake, scrub?"

"No! no!" said the girls, all at once. "We have servants to do those things."

"Can't you sew?" asked the country girl.

"Well," said one of them, "I made an apron once, but it was so poorly done that my mother had to rip it all out."

"Well," said the country girl, "I would be ashamed to be as helpless as you are—to be like a baby and have some one to wait upon me. You may talk about your fathers being worth money, but I'm worth something in myself. I can cook, wash, sew, scrub, bake and iron, and milk and make butter. I am proud of what I can do, and I never would think of boasting about what I can't do."

This country girl had a thought I would like to have you remember. It is not the amount of the money we have which measures our value. Our value is in what we are, and not in what we possess. A man may possess millions of dollars and yet be worth very little, and another may have only his two, strong hands and firm intellect, and be worth a great deal.

I want you to appreciate the value of work. Jesus says, "My Father worketh hitherto, and I work." So you see we are in good company when we are working. God knew that man, being created with Godlike qualities, would not be happy unless he was doing something, and man makes a mistake when he does not choose to do the things that are for the bettering of the world. If one's hands are occupied in honest labor, they will not be apt to get in much mischief, and even a little girl whose hands are well employed, is safer than one whose hands are idle.

But you will say that a little girl like you cannot do work of any value. It is true that your work cannot be of much value in itself, but it is of great value, because it is developing you. You are not working simply to do the work, but working to become acquainted with yourself and to "get hold" of yourself. You see the body is an instrument which we must use, and everything that we learn to do is giving us skill in the use of our bodily powers. So I like to have you learn all the work about the house; the cooking, dishwashing, sweeping, bed-making and dusting; not because you would do it better than any one else, for I could hire it done very much better than you can possibly do it at first, but because it is making you more a woman; it will make you of more use in the world.

But you say you would rather learn to use nails, saw and hammer. Well, I have no objection to your learning to use these. That also would be helpful and would develop you, but you must also learn to do those things that you do not like to do, because that will develop you even faster; for your place in the world no doubt will be as the home-maker, and there can be no more beautiful or noble work than this.

Mr. Ruskin has a very high ideal of woman, and he writes of the nature of the home. He says: "It is the place of peace, the shelter from all injury, from all terror, doubt and division, and wherever a true woman comes, this home is always round her. The stars only may be over her head, the glow worm in the night's cold grass may be the only fire at her foot, but home is wherever she is, and for a noble woman, it stretches far around her, better than ceiled with cedar or painted with vermilion, shedding its quiet light far for those who else were homeless."

Isn't that a beautiful picture of what

a woman may do in making a home, and I want you to have the ambition to be a home-maker wherever you go; to have your eyes open to see what needs to be done to make other people comfortable, to see what you can do to beautify the place, to add to the happiness of those who are in it, so whatever sphere of life you may be in, whatever position you may fill, you may make the world brighter and happier.

Mrs. Browning says:

> "Get work, get work!
> 'Tis better than what you work to get."

By this she means that the work does more for us in developing us than we accomplish for anyone else in the doing of the work itself. Our work not only builds us up bodily, but it builds up our minds. Everything which you learn to do will make you so much the more a woman. Work gives you exercise. This creates appetite; you eat heartily, your food is digested, is assimilated, and made over into yourself, and so you grow and become a strong and vigorous woman.

But you don't want all work, you want some play. Oh, yes, indeed, play is just as important as work, but it must be the right kind of play. Play should be recreation and not dissipation. We call many kinds of amusements recreation, when they are really destructive. Play, or amusement of any sort, to be of value must be of a kind that tends to build us up, rather than to destroy us.

I heard a girl say once that she was not able to walk two blocks, and yet she could dance all night without being tired. Now that is a sort of amusement that is not recreation, but dissipation, and although she did not feel tired, she must really have been injured. I knew a young man who thought he was having a fine time in visiting saloons. At the end of two weeks of dissipation he died of delirium tremens. His amusement was not recreation, but destruction.

All play or amusement should allow plenty of time for sleep, and it is much better that it be out-door amusement than indoor, in the day-time rather than in the night-time. It should be enjoyed in a proper dress. Many girls prevent themselves from being benefited by amusement by their tight clothing, an error which I am sure you will never fall into, for you understand how important it is that you should breathe sufficiently in order to have your blood purified. You cannot breathe if the centre of your body is restricted by tight clothing.

Much interest is taken nowadays in gymnastics, and that is all very well. It is right that one should practice gymnastic exercises in order to be symmetrically developed, but after all that becomes very selfish, unless one uses the strength thus attained in working, in doing something to make other people happy. I want you to be glad to be a working woman, to play with as much vigor as if you were doing something, and to work with as much interest as if you were playing, and then be able to stop both work and play and rest. I want you to be able to rest quietly, even alone, without feeling it necessary to be amused by someone else; to be able to find good company in your own thoughts. Those people are most unhappy who do not know how to be good company for themselves when alone.

TWILIGHT TALK XIV.

The Value of Books as Good Company.—How to Judge Whether a Book is Good or Bad.—The Memory a Picture Gallery.—How We Store Away Pictures of Deeds, Acts, or Words, Not Only for Ourselves, but for Others.—Wise Choice of Book Friends Desirable.—What Shall We Read?

TWILIGHT TALK XIV.

I said last evening that I want you to know how to be good company for yourself, and one of the best ways is to be interested in good reading. You can always have the best associates in good books, and with your mind stored with good ideas you always have something to think about, even when alone. As your body is nourished by the food you eat, so your mind is nourished by the books you read. You would not eat decayed fruit nor spoiled beef, and so you ought not to be willing to read anything except the best.

And how shall you judge of good reading? You can speedily tell whether the books you are reading make you desire to be better. It is not necessary that you should always read books of history, or religious books or something very sober, although you should read many books of these classes. Many stories are very good, teach good lessons, give good thoughts, and you can tell, while you are reading, whether the book makes you desire to live a nobler life, or whether it makes you think lightly of yourself, makes you think you are willing to do things that you would not care to tell mother about. Just as soon as you feel that a book or story is making you think less nobly of yourself, that is a bad book for you to read, no matter what other people may say about it. You will not let other people judge of the food you eat. You do not like tomatoes and you would not let other people feed you tomatoes, simply because they like them. You would say, "I don't like them, and I won't eat them." So in regard to books; other people may say the book is good, but if you feel that the book is not good for you, you ought not to allow anyone else to induce you to read it.

Sometimes, perhaps, a girl, or it even

may be a boy, may put into your hands something that would make you blush to read, something that you would not like to show to mother, then do not look at it yourself, do not read it, for the evil pictures which we store away in our memories make an impression far deeper and more lasting than the good pictures.

It is a wonderful thing, this picture gallery which we have in the memory. Every day, in every thing we are thinking, doing, or saying, we are putting away pictures to look at in after years. It will be well for you to remember that the pictures which you make by your own conduct are stored away in your own memory, and will also make an impression in after years upon your childdren. They may not see the same memory-pictures that you see, but an impression is made upon their characters, and they will think less nobly and purely of themselves, if you have been willing to look at pictures or read books which were degrading in any degree. You must remember that the welfare of the future rests in the hands of just such little children as you are.

If it were in your power to choose between talking with a statesman, or with some vulgar, profane man, you would not hesitate a moment to choose. It is worth a great deal to have the privilege of talking with some great person, and yet, as Ruskin says, "Here in books, it is possible for us to choose our friends, and from the very best of earth. Sometimes we may by good fortune obtain a glimpse of a great poet and hear the sound of his voice, or put a question to a man of science and be answered good-humoredly, or snatch the privilege of throwing a bouquet in the path of a princess, or arresting the kind glance of a queen; * * * but, meantime, there is a society continually open to us of people who will talk to us as long as we like, whatever our rank or occupation, talk to us in the best words they can choose and with thanks, if we listen to them. And this society, because it is so numerous and so gentle and can be kept waiting around us all day long, not to grant audience, but to gain it—kings and statesmen lingering patiently in those plainly furnished and narrow ante-rooms, our bookcase shelves, we make no account of that company—perhaps never listen to a word they would say all day long."

And just think of it! That company is just as willing to talk to you, a little girl, as to talk to the greatest man in the world; so you can choose your associates among the best and noblest of earth, be with them to-day, to-morrow, and all the days, and they are never impatient with you, they never refuse to repeat over and over again the things you want them to say, they will say it to you to-day and to-morrow just as patiently It is a wonderful fact that we can thus bring into our lives the best and purest of earth, to hear their words of wisdom and learn from them.

I have seen girls and boys who were great readers, but they didn't seem to choose their friends, their book-friends, very wisely. They like to associate with robbers, and thieves, and pirates, and bandits, in scenes of murder and robbery and intrigue. It seems strange, doesn't it? They are storing away in their memories things that they ought not to remember; indeed, they are spoiling their memories by filling them so full of things not worth remembering.

Read histories and biographies, read about the sciences and art, read of travel and exploration, read about morals and religion, but do not read stories and trash. The world is too full of good books, there are too many things in the realm of the actual and the real, concerning which you cannot afford to be ignorant, to permit the reading of worthless books.

TWILIGHT TALK XV.

Friendships, Their Value.—Friendships Between Boys and Girls.—Girlish Intimacies.—Same Standard of Conduct for Both Sexes.—"Sowing Wild Oats."—Cannot be Too Choice in Companionship.—We are Souls Expressing Ourselves Through Bodies.—One Soul Lives in Man's Body, Another lives in Woman's Body, but Both are Souls.—The Influence of Young Girls.—Thoughts Weave Garments for Us.

TWILIGHT TALK XV.

In one of our talks I said I did not like to hear little boys and girls teased about being lovers and sweethearts, and to-night I want to talk to you about the friendship of children. You asked me if I did not think it well for girls to be friends with boys. Yes, I would like you to have friends among boys, the same as friends among good girls; but you should be just as careful in your choice of boy-friends as in your choice of girl-friends. I do not like even to see little girls too intimate. Each should have enough self-respect to keep her own secrets, or have her secret with her mother.

I have known little girls who had no idea of keeping family affairs to themselves, and would tell to their little girl-friends things that happened in the home, which should not have been talked about. As one little girl said, "We have only six spoons at our house. When we have company mother has to go without or I have to wait." Now, of course it was no disgrace, if they were poor, to have only six spoons, but it would be a mortification to the mother to have it told through the neighborhood. One little girl was asked by a gentleman if she knew what her father's price was for a certain piece of property. She said, "He asks $6000, but he will take $5000." So by her thoughtless telling what she had heard at home, she lost her father a good sale.

I believe that little girls should have self-respect, and keep every one at a proper distance, both physically and otherwise. It doesn't look well to see girls and women kissing each other in public places, and it certainly is not right that girls and boys should be kissing each other either publicly or privately. If ever there is a kiss or caress received by a little girl that she does not want to tell mother about that is certainly one that she should not have received. Little girls should learn to be dignified and have self-respect, not allowing anyone familiarity or freedom. I am always sorry when I see little girls caressed and fondled by men. It often makes the little girls bold in their conduct, and certainly destroys the bloom of purity and self-respect.

There is another matter, very important to the welfare of the whole world, and yet which I think you can comprehend. It is the necessity of men and boys being as careful of their conduct as are women and girls.

We sometimes hear people making excuses for boys and young men who are dissipated or profane or immoral. They say, "Oh, he's a boy. He must have his fling! He'll settle down by and by and be all the better for having 'sowed his wild oats.'"

You never hear people talk in this way of girls. If a young woman should visit the saloon, and smoke cigars and swear, no one would ever excuse her by saying, "Oh, she must 'have her fling.' She'll settle down by and by and be the better for having 'sowed her wild oats.'" Oh, no! Everybody feels that a stain on the character of a girl cannot be removed. She is taught from her earliest childhood that because she is a girl she must be careful in her conduct and pure in her speech. She must not associate with bad girls, nor go to bad places. And yet she is not taught that it is just as important that the boy should live purely, nor is she required to be as careful in her association with boys as with girls.

The girl who would visit saloons or smoke is not fit to go in good society, but the boy who does these, and much more, is too often invited into the most cultured families as an honored guest. This is all wrong, and if all girls would begin now to say by their conduct that they believe boys ought to be just as pure and good as girls, it would soon change public opinion. Boys think they can do all sorts of wrong things and it will make no difference; girls will be just as glad to see them, to go with them, to receive any attention from them. Too often young women are willing to marry such young men. But these young men would not be willing to marry girls whose characters were as vile as their own.

You cannot be too choice in your companionship, and you should choose your boy-friends with just the same care that you do your girl-friends. You should make them feel that if they are to have your friendship they must be noble, good and true, just as they expect you to be.

I think we can understand why boys should be as pure and good as girls when we remember that we are souls, living in and expressing ourselves through bodies, and it is as souls that our conduct is to be judged. What one soul does is of just as much importance as what any other soul does. It is in God's sight no less a hideous sin for boys to swear or be impure than for girls, for God looks at us as souls. He knows that the body does only what the soul prompts it to do. It is not the body that is guilty. The body does not lie or swear. It is the soul that expresses itself through the organs of speech. The body is in itself not vile, but the soul, tainted with vile thoughts and evil desires, moves the body to do its bidding. The body is our house. Does the style of house one lives in change the quality of his deeds? Is it any less sinful for the person who lives in a gray house to steal than for one who lives in a white house. We would think it a strange way to judge of conduct to say, "Oh, Mr. L. may steal and lie. He lives in a gray house, and it is the nature of people who live in gray houses to do that way; but Mr. A. ought not to steal or lie for he lives in a white house, and it is expected that those who live in white houses should be honest and upright." We would know at once that the kind or color of the house makes no difference, has no effect on the quality of his conduct.

This is just as true in regard to our bodily dwelling. One soul lives in the body of a man, another lives in the body of a woman, but both are souls, and one just as much responsible for right conduct as the other. Therefore, there is no more excuse for a man's doing wrong than for a woman's doing wrong; God's law is the same for both. What you would not excuse in your girl-friend you should not excuse in your boy-friend. What you know is right for yourself will be just as right for little brother, and I should be just as sorry to see him soiled with evil thoughts and deeds as I should be to see you thus soiled.

Even as a little girl you can help to make public opinion. You have your own place of influence among your little circle of friends. Live up to your highest thoughts and help your companions, boys and girls, to do the same, and you will have had an influence on the moral condition of the world in years to come.

I knew a girl in my childhood who was very careful of her own conduct, and although she did not say much in correction of the rest of us, she made us better just by the atmosphere of goodness that was around her. I overheard two boys talking about her, and one said, "I don't know why it is, but somehow I never can feel an evil thought or speak a wrong word in Clara's presence. She always makes me feel that I want to be just as good as I can possibly be, although she does not talk goodness."

"No," said the other, "she just lives goodness and it sweetens the air all around her."

I read a poem once that said "Thoughts are things," and it would really seem as if it were true, wouldn't it. Our thoughts, Dr. Gates says, create actual substances in our blood, and it seems as if they go out from us and surround us with an atmosphere that is felt by others. We clothe ourselves in a garment of thought, and people recognize this and know us by our thought-clothing.

You know how irritated you feel when Mrs. Blake comes here, even though she treats you pleasantly. You feel that her thought is of a quality that stirs you up and makes you feel cross. When you were sick you were always worse after she called, although she tried very hard to be kind and pleasant. But Mrs. Clark's influence was very different. You said you felt better the minute she came into the door. She did not say much to you, but you felt her thought-atmosphere, and were quieted.

We may let other people buy our clothes for us, and so what we wear may not tell much about our taste or character; but our thought-garments we weave for ourselves, and those who come into contact with us must feel what we really are. The girl who is dressed in silk and finery may have a very coarse thought-garment, while the girl whose poverty compels her to dress in plain calico may be so sweet and pure and true that she is clothed in the richest thought-dress, and her nobility of soul makes itself recognized by all.

TWILIGHT TALK XVI.

What it is to Become a Woman.—The Bodily Changes at that Time.—Organs Not Fully Developed.—Should Have Time to Grow.—The Girl the Bud of the Woman.—New Mental Emotions to be Guarded.—Housework Good Exercise.

TWILIGHT TALK XVI.

You have been looking forward with much interest to the time when you would be a woman. You think it will be the time when you will wear long dresses, coil up your braids of hair, go into society, and do pretty much as you please, but all these things will not make you a woman. Something more is needed than to grow tall, to leave school and have a "coming-out party."

Certain bodily changes must take place in order that you may be a woman. You will not only grow taller, but your figure will become fuller, your voice sweeter, you will care less for your hoydenish plays, but will be more gentle and ladylike. And in addition to these outward signs, other changes will be taking place inside your body. As yet your reproductive organs have been asleep. There has been no need for them. When you are about fourteen years old they will wake up and begin to take on activity, and then will be the time when the outward signs I have spoken of will appear. These outward signs are only manifestations of what is taking place inwardly.

The reproductive organs of the woman are the sac in which the baby finds its home, the ovary where the egg or germ was developed, with the muscles that hold these in place, and the passage leading up to them. They are all located at the very lower part of the body, where they are well protected. The girl at fourteen is said to have reached the age of puberty, which means, the time when hair begins to grow on the body, as in the armpits, or over the parts beneath which are the reproductive organs; but we use the word as denoting that she has passed through the physical change which makes her a woman, that she has reached the age when it is possible for her to become a mother. But these organs are not fully developed, and will need years in which to grow strong and ready for the work of child-bearing. Girls do sometimes marry at fourteen or fifteen and become mothers, but it is a great mistake to do so, for it is injurious to their own health, and their children can never be as strong as if the mother had had time to become more firm in her bodily organs. You know how it is with the flower-buds. You can sometimes pull them apart and make them look like a full-blown flower, but they fade very soon, and the beauty of the bud is lost altogether.

The bud needs to grow and unfold, and when left to do this in accordance with its nature will become a perfect full-blown flower. The girl is the bud of the woman, and she needs time to blossom out in perfect loveliness. She should be willing to allow nature to work slowly. She should be glad to be the beautiful human bud as long as is possible, for after the flower has blown it can never go back and be the bud again, and the earlier the bud becomes the flower, the sooner will it wither and decay. Unfortunately, girls are not always wisely taught in regard to themselves and, not understanding what all these changes mean, they are too anxious to reach the full stage of womanhood.

Along with the physical changes come new mental emotions and feelings, which the girl does not understand. She feels a strange weariness, perhaps headache or backache. She is nervous, it may be irritable, and inclined to cry over little things, or even about nothing. This is the time when the girl needs to be patient with herself, as well as to receive kindly consideration from others. If she understands what all these things mean, she will not be disturbed, but will say to herself, "I am getting to be a woman."

At this time in her life the girl needs to be more careful of her health than before. She should use good judgment in her exercise or amusement, though it is not needful for her to think herself an invalid. She should be out of doors a great deal, and have "real good times," only she should be careful not to overdo, and especially should she secure plenty of good, sound sleep every night. At this time in her life she needs to remember all that she has been taught in regard to care of her bodily health. A little housework is very good occupation, and girls can learn to do these homely duties with pleasure if they remember that good housekeeping is a part of successful home-making. Dish-washing is especially beneficial, as the hot water calls the blood to the hands and so helps to relieve the headache or backache.

I heard a lady tell the other day how she would make dishwashing a delight. She said, "I would say, this hot water represents truth, heated by love. The soiled dishes represent myself, with all my worn-out thoughts and desires. I plunge them in the loving truth and cleanse them thoroughly, then polish them with the towel of persistence and store them away in symmetrical order to await further use. So I myself am warmed and interested, and my work is well done."

George Herbert says:

"A servant, with this clause,
  Makes drudgery divine,
Who sweeps a room as for God's laws,
  Makes that, and the action fine."

It is far better for the young girl at puberty to be gently active in household duties than to be lying around reading romances. These exciting stories do her great harm, physical as well as mental. They are like forcing houses that hurry the buds into blossoms. Many little girls are being hurried into the physical development of womanhood through novel-reading. I want you to be my little girl as long as you can, and, therefore, I ask you not to read love-stories and silly books of romance. There are so many beautiful books nowadays for young people that you can find plenty of healthful reading. And nature is the most delightful book of all. Read the lives of plants and flowers as they grow in the garden, read the experiences of the living birds in the trees. Learn to know their songs, so that you recognize them whenever you hear them. I know a young girl who keeps an opera glass always at hand and I have often seen her jump up from the dinner table, catch up the glass and rush out to examine some bird whose song was new to her.

To be interested in home duties and in nature is the safest pleasure for the young girl. It diverts her mind from herself, and so she forgets the new emotions that come as a part of her development.

Too often at this time of life girls become sentimental and think they should go into society and have beaux. Sometimes they even show an inclination to "run after the boys," as they say. This is because the dear girl does not understand herself. She does not know that the new feelings she experiences are due to the awakening of her sexual nature, that she should now be even more, rather than less, guarded in her companionship. She should more carefully shun personal familiarities, for they brush off the bloom of perfect innocence, as rough handling brushes the dew from the flower, and nothing can ever restore it.

There are some physical changes which take place at puberty of which I will more fully tell you as the time approaches. Meanwhile, I want you to be my happy little girl, enjoying every day with that kind of pleasure that you will be glad to remember through all your life, and which you would be perfectly willing to have known to the world, or repeated to your children.

The End.

www.ingramcontent.com/pod-product-compliance
Lightning Source LLC
Chambersburg PA
CBHW021728220426
43662CB00008B/753